DORSET RAILWAYS

DORSET RAILWAYS

COLIN G. MAGGS

DORSET BOOKS

First published in Great Britain in 2009

British Library Cataloguing-in-Publication Data
A CIP record for this title is available from the British Library

ISBN 978 1 871164 66 4

DORSET BOOKS
Dorset Books is a Partnership Between
Dorset County Council & Halsgrove

Halsgrove House,
Ryelands Industrial Estate,
Bagley Road, Wellington, Somerset TA21 9PZ
Tel: 01823 653777   Fax: 01823 216796
email: sales@halsgrove.com

Part of the Halsgrove group of companies
Information on all Halsgrove titles is available at: www.halsgrove.com

Printed and bound in Great Britain by CPI Antony Rowe Ltd., Wiltshire

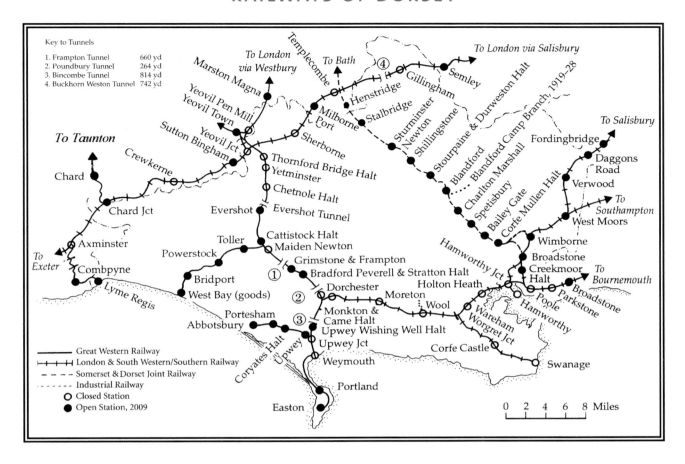

Key to Tunnels
1. Frampton Tunnel   660 yd
2. Poundbury Tunnel   264 yd
3. Bincombe Tunnel   814 yd
4. Buckhorn Weston Tunnel 742 yd

—————— Great Western Railway
+-+-+-+- London & South Western/Southern Railway
– – – –   Somerset & Dorset Joint Railway
· · · · · · Industrial Railway
○ Closed Station
● Open Station, 2009

0 2 4 6 8 Miles

Contents

1 An Outline Survey of Railways in Dorset

T HE FIRST railway in Dorset was not a steam operated line, but one worked by horses and gravity. In the early nineteenth century there was an increasing demand for Portland stone and an economic means was required for transporting it from quarries on top of the island down to a jetty. Unlike many such contemporary lines, an Act of Parliament was sought for the line's construction. This obtained Royal Assent on 10 June 1825. Unlike many lines which found difficulty in raising the necessary finance, even before the Bill was passed £5,000 had been subscribed, exceeding the estimated cost by £310 8s 0d.

The line, the Merchants' Railway, opened by October 1826 and between that month and 31 December 1826 4,803 tons of stone were carried. Stone was brought to the railway by horse drawn carts, craned into wagons on the 4ft 6in gauge railway, drawn by horses to the head of the incline where the trucks

descended by gravity, a cable round a drum at the top of the incline enabling empty wagons to be drawn up the incline. The cable section was known colloquially as 'The Blondin' after the famous tightrope walker.

The inclined plane was in two sections: 303yd and 282yd. Subsequently quarry owners laid lines from their quarries to the Merchants' Railway. The line paid its shareholders good dividends – 7½ per cent for the first six months of 1939, but with the outbreak of World War 2 almost all quarrying ceased and the line closed on 11 October 1939, though the track was not lifted until 1958. Its peak year was 1904 when 93,133 tons were carried.

In 1848 construction started on another gravity worked railway to bring stone to build a breakwater, the quarrying of stone being by convicts from the nearby prison. This incline had three sections and its gauge was 7ft. At the foot of the incline, two steam locomotives drew wagons to the breakwater.

The first main line in the county was the Southampton & Dorchester which opened on 1 June 1847. The next main line in Dorset was the Wilts, Somerset & Weymouth Railway (WSWR). This line was planned to link the Great Western Railway (GWR) near Chippenham with Weymouth. It received its Act in 1845, but due to the slump following the Railway Mania, investment was slow and it did not reach Weymouth until 20 January 1857. The Southampton & Dorchester Railway had running power over the line between Dorchester and Weymouth and opened to Weymouth on 20 January 1857.

The Salisbury & Yeovil Railway opened to Gillingham on 2 May 1859, to Yeovil on 1 June 1860, and onwards to Exeter on 19 July 1860. The Dorset Central Railway was inaugurated between Wimborne and Blandford on 1 November 1860 and northwards to Cole on 3 February 1862 where it linked

A loaded stone wagon descending the quarry railway at Portland. The cable attached to the wagon passes round a drum behind the photographer and proceeds down the left-hand track to an empty wagon towards the foot of the incline, which it is drawing up. The centre rail is common to both tracks but in the middle of the incline branches to two tracks to enable the wagons to pass. M. J. Tozer collection

with the Somerset Central Railway, the two companies uniting as the Somerset & Dorset Railway. The extension to Bath opened 20 July 1874 creating a new main line.

Thus was established the pattern of four main lines in Dorset: two running approximately east to west and two north to south. From these main lines, branches were created to serve places off a main line such as to Lyme Regis, Bridport, Abbotsbury, Portland and Swanage. Although very useful in the days of horse-drawn traffic, the more convenient internal-combustion engined vehicles rendered these branches uneconomic and they were closed around the time of the 1963 Beeching Report.

2 How a Railway was Created

IN THE 19th century businessmen and landowners wishing to improve trade, increase the value of their property and invest their cash profitably might propose a scheme for linking two places by a railway. The way they went about such a scheme followed a general pattern which can be described once and serve to tell the story of the creation of almost any railway in Dorset. Several meetings would be called in the locality and provided that sufficient financial support was promised, a bill would be placed before Parliament, itself often proving an expensive process. Committees of the houses of Commons and Lords received evidence for and against the proposed line. If both houses passed the bill it became an Act of Parliament and the promoting company was then legally entitled to raise a stipulated sum of money to purchase land and build the railway between the two chosen places. Before going to Parliament a surveyor would have drawn up plans. Ideally, a line would be straight, level, and pass through or close to chief settlements, yet using cheaper, rather than expensive land. If tunnels, cuttings and embankments were required, the surveyor would

Surveyors at work.
F.S. Williams

9

endeavour to make sure that soil excavated could be used in a nearby embankment. Those plans, known as Deposited Plans, were placed with the local authority and Parliament. After the passing of the Act and the capital raised, a contractor had to be found to carry out the work; those companies with less money would seek one willing to work for shares rather than for cash.

Work usually began with the ceremonial turning of the first turf, a highly decorated spade being used to lift the sod into an equally ornate wheelbarrow. That was often done by the company's chairman or his wife. After the ceremony the directors and local dignitaries dined. The contractor set to work and was likely to meet difficulties - a shortage of workers or materials, hard rock in an unexpected place that had to be cut through, or fluid clay that refused to stay in place. The railway company might be unable to raise enough money to pay the contractor or the contractor himself might go bankrupt. Parliament wisely decided that a railway company must deposit a sum of money so that in the event of failure to complete the line after work had started, the money deposited could be used to re-instate the property purchased compulsorily from the landowners. The Act of Parliament stipulated that a line should be completed within a certain period of time and quite often, because of various difficulties, the railway was forced to apply to Parliament for an extension of time and not infrequently for an increase in capital to cover unforeseen costs.

When the contractor completed the line and before it could be opened to passenger traffic, an inspection had to be undertaken for the Board of Trade through an officer of the Royal Engineers. He went over the line testing bridges and other structures, making sure that the signalling was adequate for safety and the stations had suitable facilities. Usually at least one fault was discovered. If it was minor the Board of Trade granted a certificate subject to its correction; if there was major criticism, re-inspection was required before the line could be opened.

On the opening day the directors and local dignitaries travelled over the line, dining afterwards. If the railway was a local one, it was usually worked by a larger company to make the business more economic. That was because,

Spoil is brought to the end of an embankment and tipped.
F.S.Williams

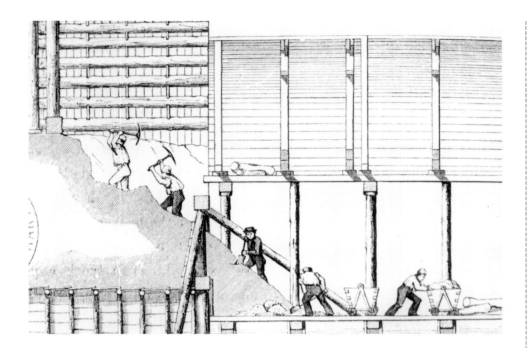

although perhaps the line might require only one engine and two passenger coaches to work services, at least one more engine would be needed as a spare when the other engine was having a boiler wash-out or undergoing repair. On market days, fair days and Bank Holidays two coaches might prove insufficient. Some goods traffic required special rolling stock and it would not be sensible to invest capital in something used only occasionally. To obviate such difficulties a small company therefore usually arranged for a larger company with larger resources to work the line for a percentage of the gross receipts. Some lines were far from profitable, ordinary shareholders rarely or never receiving a dividend, and it often happened that eventually a small railway was purchased by the working company, the payment usually less than its building cost.

Particularly if it was a branch line, it probably suffered from bus competition in the 1920s, buses being more convenient as passengers could board nearer their homes and be dropped nearer their destinations. Railway stations tended to be built at locations convenient from the railway's point of view, quite often some distance from a village or town centre. To help combat bus competition, unstaffed halts were opened at points near to centres of population.

In the early 1900s railmotors came into use. A railmotor was a passenger coach and locomotive contained on the same underframe. It was designed so that when going boiler-first the engine would be at the front but when returning the driver could walk to what had been the rear and drive from a special control compartment, the fireman remaining at the other end. The use of a railmotor obviated the time and trouble needed to run an engine round its train at the end of every journey. When a railmotor service was introduced, unmanned halts were opened at places where traffic was insufficient to warrant a staffed station.

Railmotors were found to lack flexibility. If, on (say) a market day, the number of passengers quadrupled, a railmotor could not cope as it was only powerful enough to draw one trailer. As a railway had to have a locomotive and

Bricking a tunnel.
F.W. Simms

coaches standing by for such an eventuality, then any saving made by the railmotor was lost.

The solution was a push-pull or auto train. An engine stayed at one end of the train and on the return journey the driver could control his engine from a special compartment at what had been the rear by means of mechanical rods or compressed air.

The year 1923 brought Grouping when, apart from very minor lines, all railway companies became part of one of the Big Four: the Great Western Railway (GWR), the London, Midland & Scottish Railway (LMS); the London & North Eastern Railway (LNER) and the Southern Railway (SR). The GWR was the only railway to retain its old name, the London & South Western Railway becoming part of the SR and the Midland Railway part of the LMS. The

Somerset & Dorset Joint Railway was unaffected by Grouping and continued to be run as a joint line but its owners changed from the Midland Railway and the London & South Western Railway to the LMS and SR. With Nationalisation on 1 January 1948 the GWR became British Railways, Western Region, and the SR the Southern Region, though minor area changes were made.

Railways were quick to spot the bus competitor and themselves participated in road transport, the GWR owning its first bus in 1903 though its first service in Dorset, from Wyke Regis to Weymouth and Radipole was not inaugurated until 22 June 1905. The London & South Western Railway operated several services from Weymouth jointly with the GWR.

From 1928 legislation permitted railways to purchase large, but not controlling, shareholdings in existing bus companies. The GWR and SR reached agreement with the National Omnibus & Transport Company: the Western National was set up to run bus services in GWR territory, the railway agreeing to transfer its road motor services to that company in return for a half share, the Western National undertaking to co-ordinate rail and road services and not to compete with the railway. The Southern National operated similar services in the SR area.

In addition to bus competition, the increase in private car ownership in the 1950s and the 1960s was another reason for the decline in the number of rail passengers and many of the poorly frequented stations closed. The smaller stations remaining open were generally unstaffed, passengers purchasing their tickets from the conductor guard on the diesel multiple unit pay trains. Freight traffic also declined because of increased use of road vehicles, especially at times when railwaymen were on strike, their actions permanently damaging business. The swing to the use of electricity, North Sea gas and oil for heating brought a decrease in the once very heavy coal traffic to almost every station. Forty five years ago railways carried relatively small loads to a variety of destinations; today the railways are the only bulk carriers of stone, steel, cars, coal and oil.

Southampton &
Dorchester Railway
seal. Author's
collection

S&DJR 4-4-0 No
18 at Branksome
shed. This engine
was painted in the
company's dark
blue livery.
Author's collection

3 The London & South Western Main Line to Weymouth

T HE SOUTHAMPTON & Dorchester Railway Act passed on 21 July 1845 authorised a capital of £500,000 and allowed the railway to be leased to the LSWR, it being usual for a relatively small railway to be worked by a larger

S&DJR Class 7F 2-8-0 No 53808 and London, Brighton & South Coast Railway 4-4-2 No 32424 *Beachy Head* at Branksome, 12 October 1957. It was a rare sight to observe a Southern engine at this shed and even rarer to see one from the LBSCR. Author's collection

company rather than purchase its own locomotives and rolling stock. The LSWR absorbed the Southampton & Dorchester on 11 October 1848.

The Southampton & Dorchester travelled via Brockenhurst and Ringwood, Bournemouth then being an insignificant place. This line was known as 'Castleman's Corkscrew' or 'The Water Snake' due to its many twists, because the Commissioners of Woods and Forests made the railway deviate around the New Forest. Charles Castleman, a Wimborne solicitor, was the chairman of the company. At Dorchester the railway was permitted to connect with the Wilts, Somerset & Weymouth Railway built to the broad gauge of 7ft 0¼ in, whereas the Southampton & Dorchester was built to the now standard gauge of 4ft 8½in. In return for laying mixed gauge between Dorchester and Weymouth, the Wilts, Somerset & Weymouth insisted on the LSWR laying broad gauge rails for eight miles eastwards towards Wareham and this strange mixed gauge section ended, apparently uselessly, out in the wilds.

Lack of heavy engineering works enabled the Southampton & Dorchester to be constructed rapidly and the 60½ miles were built in less than two years – excellent progress when one remembers that all spoil had to be shifted manually. Peto, the contractor, was offered a £5,000 bonus to complete the works by 1 May 1847, the LSWR agreeing to wooden bridges being built for speed. When building the line, seven navvies were killed and ten suffered serious injury. On 25 May 1847 a trial train consisting of three carriages, a horse box and three wagons of signalling equipment for distribution along the line, left Bletchynden, now Southampton Central, at 5.30 am and arrived at Dorchester five hours later. The return was made in three hours.

The line was opened publicly on Tuesday 1 June 1847, but from Bletchynden, not Southampton Terminus station, as the intervening tunnel had collapsed two nights before. Peto had filled in a disused canal crossing the railway tunnel with rubble in order to satisfy the owners of the property above and this damming caused water from the canal tunnel seeking to escape, to saturate the clay above the railway tunnel until it collapsed. Horse buses linked the two stations until 6

The attractive canopy support on the up platform at Branksome, 19 September 1986. Author

The ornate road bridge at Parkstone, view up, 19 September 1986. Author

August when the tunnel was reopened. This incident caused confusion and on 1 June a notice announcing postponement of opening was fixed on the doors of Ringwood station, but was hastily removed when the first train arrived. Five trains ran each way daily over the single line, the fastest taking two hours fifty five minutes and the slowest 3¼ hours.

Unfortunately a head-on collision occurred on 27 September 1847. As the last down train was passing over the points at Wool, two coaches and a brake van were derailed. A messenger was sent to Wareham for assistance and in the flurry the stationmaster there misunderstood and thought that the up mail train had been derailed and sent out the contractor's engine to assist. Meanwhile at Wool the down train had been re-railed and left for Dorchester and on its arrival

An up LSWR passenger train at Parkstone station. It carries a diamond and disc headcode. Author's collection

there, the up mail departed and met the contractor's engine in the deep, curved cutting at Worgret, 1½ miles from Wareham. Fortunately no lives were lost.

Although the Southampton and Dorchester Act gave running powers over the WSWR from Dorchester to Weymouth, the WSWR was unable to complete this line until 20 January 1857, so the LSWR could not reach Weymouth until this date.

The LSWR's layout at Dorchester station was strange because it allowed for an extension to Exeter which was never built. Down trains from Southampton to Weymouth used a platform on the sharp curve which led to the WSWR line, but up trains had to negotiate the curve and then set back into the terminal platforms covered by a train shed until its removal circa 1938. This time-wasting procedure lasted for over 120 years until 28 June 1970 when an up platform was built on the through line. The line was electrified on 6 October 1986 and on 14 April 1988 the fastest train ever to run from Waterloo to Weymouth covered the distance in 1 hour 59 minutes 24 seconds.

Dorchester station was very busy on 4 August 1849 when the first cheap day excursion ran to Southampton. Although departure was at 5.00am, no less than 21 coaches and 49 open wagons had to be provided to accommodate all the passengers. The two engines stabled at Dorchester having insufficient tractive

Two LMS Class 4F 0-6-0s No 44100 and No 43875 at Parkstone head a stopping train to Bournemouth West on Saturday 5 August 1950. No 44100 is from Burton shed. The S&D was short of locomotives on summer Saturdays and No 44100 would have arrived at Bath on a goods from the north and then worked to Bournemouth ready to head a train of returning holidaymakers. S.W.Baker

The attractive Parkstone station 19 September 1986, view down. The up road has been electrified. Author

S&D Class 7F 2-8-0 No 53804 descends Parkstone Bank with a Bournemouth West to Bath express, 2 August 1952. The single line tablet catcher can be seen towards the front of the tender. S.W.Baker

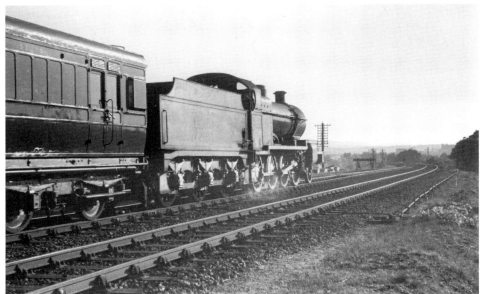

Poole, view down circa 1860 before doubling. The crossing keeper's cottage is on the left. Author's collection

Poole, East signal box left, view down circa 1939. Author's collection

power, the goods engine on a London stone train was commandeered and the excursion left at 5.18 behind three locomotives. It returned to Dorchester nearly 24 hours later at 2.10am, when the stationmaster and staff had to rouse the sleeping excursionists from the coaches needed for ordinary services, but those in the open wagons were left undisturbed. London apparently failed to inquire why its stone train was a day overdue.

Twenty-five years later a rather interesting mixed train ran between Weymouth and Southampton Docks. A maximum of four coaches could be attached

Class 9F 2-10-0 No 92233 heads a Bournemouth West to Bath train through Poole circa 1960. Bryan H.Jackson

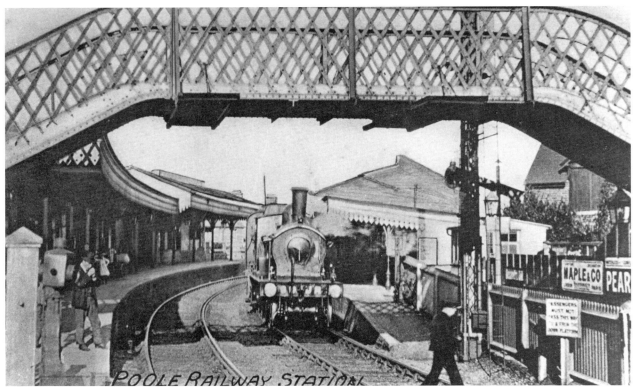

A Johnson S&D 4-4-0 at Poole heads an S&D train to Bournemouth West circa 1900. The notice on the right reads: Passengers must not cross this way to and from the down platform. Notice the shields below the bridge to prevent users suffering ill effects from smoke and cinders. Author's collection

West Country class Pacific No 34028 *Eddystone* heads an up train at Poole. Dr T.R.N.Edwards

S&D 4-4-0 No 71 heads an express from the Midlands to Bournemouth West at Poole, 1914. 'S&D' on the buffer beam was unusual, 'SDJR' being the normal format. Author's collection

An S&D Class 7F 2-8-0 at Poole heads an express to the North circa 1950. Notice the check rails on the tight curve. D.W. Law

An up stopping train headed by M7 class 0-4-4T No 30111 enters Poole, 3 July 1954. R.E.Toop/Author's collection

The very bland new buildings on the up platform, Poole, 1 May 1986. Author

behind the good wagons. 4 hours 40 minutes was allowed for the distance of 63½ miles. Despite this apparently generous allowance, shunting en route took so long that in May 1874, although the scheduled time for arrival was 10.25pm, Southampton was reached at times varying between 10.41pm and 1.29am.

In practice it was found that the station platforms were too short, so their extension to 250ft began in 1858 concurrent with doubling the track. Double track reached Dorchester on 1 August 1863.

An interesting feature seen at Bryer Ash's coal office at Dorchester and protected by an iron railing, was a large lump of coal from Kilmersdon Colliery near Radstock. It measured approximately 9ft x 5ft x 5ft.

Four miles east of Dorchester a siding for the Airship Station opened in May 1918 while the nearby Airship Station Halt opened in 1919 and closed circa 1923. From Moreton station a line led to gravel pits on the south side and a brick yard to the north. East of the station the UK Atomic Energy authority's Winfrith Sidings opened on 6 October 1974. The next station bore the imaginative nameboard 'Wool for Lulworth Cove'. In 1919 a goods line built by prisoners-of-war was opened to the Royal Tank Corps depot at Bovington and continued to operate until 1928, the track being lifted for scrap in 1936.

West of Wareham the line crosses the River Piddle on an iron span with two red brick arches, this being a Grade II listed bridge. It was designed by the Southampton & Dorchester engineer Captain W.S.Moorsom. Wareham station was originally east of the level crossing, but in order to cope with the opening of the Swanage branch, an attractive new four platform station, now Grade II listed, was built to the west and opened on 4 April 1887, one of the gables bearing the LSWR coat of arms. Rather unusually the signals at Wareham were

Robert Stephenson & Hawthorns Ltd Works No 7544 of 1949 Bonnie Prince Charlie, shunter at Southern Wharves Ltd, Poole, 26 August 1954. The car on the right deserves a second glance. Revd Alan Newman

Tracks at Poole Quay. Author's collection

Hamworthy Junction, view down, 1965. J.H. Lucking

lit by town gas rather than by oil, but circa 1908 were replaced by Coligny-Welch long burning oil lamps which saved approximately £8 a month.

Around 1900 the 8.45am from Weymouth was only allowed 15 minutes for the 14 miles 79 chains from Dorchester to Wareham, necessitating an average speed of over 60mph. To meet this schedule, speeds of 80mph were required on down gradients. One driver was fined £2 plus three days suspension for working the distance in 14 minutes and causing one of his engine's axleboxes to overheat. In postwar years, Bulleid's Pacifics were fast enough to exceed 'even time' in the opposite and uphill direction.

East of Wareham, until 10 December 1967, Sandford Siding served a pottery, while further east at Keysworth, one siding led to a gravel pit and another was for military use. The austere Holton Heath station opened for workers at the Admiralty cordite factory on 3 April 1916 and to the public on 14 July 1924. Circa 1989 5 acres of this site, now the Holton Heath Industrial estate, became a railhead. At Hamworthy Junction a line comes in from Hamworthy Goods and at the east end of the station, the line diverged to Broadstone and Poole.

Continuing along the 'Old Road' towards Broadstone, two clay sidings adjoined Lytchett Crossing signal box. East of Wimborne, Uddens Estate Siding

King Arthur class 4-6-0 No 737 *King Uther* passes Hamworthy Junction with a Waterloo to Weymouth train, July 1948. C.T. Standfast

The stark Holton Heath station, view up, 15 April 1967. Author

was taken out of use on 8 June 1943 when a Government siding was opened on the opposite side of the line. East of West Moors a War Department depot opened on 14 February 1943, beyond which the line passed into Hampshire.

To complete the story, Bournemouth grew into an important watering place and a new line between Brockenhurst and Poole via Bournemouth was opened on 6 March 1888, the former main line via Ringwood and Wimborne becoming a mere branch and finally much of it closing on 4 May 1964. The new main line caused Bournemouth to grow very rapidly indeed.

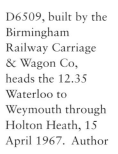

D6509, built by the Birmingham Railway Carriage & Wagon Co, heads the 12.35 Waterloo to Weymouth through Holton Heath, 15 April 1967. Author

33 109 propels 4-TC set No 428 through Holton Heath working the 13.34 Weymouth to Waterloo, 1 May 1986. The driver controls the engine, which is at the rear of the train, from the cab at the leading end of the formation. A 'bus stop' type shelter has replaced the larger structure. Insulators lie on the permanent way ready for electrification. Author

Wareham station view up, 15 April 1967. A Swanage train stands on the right in the bay platform. Notice the loudspeaker fixed to the swan-necked lamp post. Beyond the level crossing at the far end of the platform, tankers stand in the goods yard. Author

The attractive entrance to Wareham station, 15 April 1967, with the LSWR crest carved above the doorway. Author

The interesting nameboard, 29 August 1968. Author

Wool station, view up, 15 April 1967. Pullman camping coaches stand on the left. The concrete lamp posts were cast by the SR at Exmouth Junction. It would not be a pleasant experience crossing the footbridge in a howling gale. Author

Moreton station from the east, 15 April 1967. Author

West Country class Pacific No 34013 *Okehampton* east of Moreton with the 12.10 Weymouth to Bournemouth train, 15 April 1967. The load will not tax this large locomotive. Author

Moreton station view up, 1 May 1986, showing the 'bus stop' type shelter. The line of notices reads: Caution: mind the step when alighting from train. Author

The interior of Moreton signal box. Author's collection

Woodsford automatic level crossing barrier, 15 April 1967. The gates were replaced by automatic half-barriers on 15 September 1965 rendering the crossing keeper in the cottage on the left, redundant. Author

A view of Dorchester station 1847. Author's collection

The exterior of Dorchester South, 4 August 1981. Author

A general view of the LSWR station at Dorchester circa 1900. The terminal platform is covered by a train shed; the sharply curved down platform used by Weymouth trains is centre-right; and on the far right is the locomotive shed. Author's collection

Dorchester South 1955: the curved down platform left and the straight up platform with its train shed removed circa 1938, on the far right. Dr A.J.G. Dickens

King Arthur class
4-6-0 No 30743
Lyonesse heads an
up stopping train at
Dorchester South, 20
September 1952. The
former train shed's
roof supports can be
seen on the left. The
plate bearing the
number '121' denotes
the number of the
bridge – the subway
below it linking the
two platforms.
A.E.West

Dorchester South
view up, 4 August
1981. Notice that
the right hand rail
of each track has a
checkrail: this is
common on sharp
curves. Author

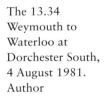

The 13.34
Weymouth to
Waterloo at
Dorchester South,
4 August 1981.
Author

The tall signal box at Dorchester South, left, and West Country class Pacific No 34095 *Brentor* outside the locomotive shed circa 1955. The shed closed 17 June 1957. The lines to and from Weymouth passed to the left of the signal box. Notice the fire buckets hanging from the signal box wall – a very necessary precaution with a timber building in the vicinity of steam locomotives. Dr A.J.G.Dickens

Dorchester South circa 1955. The goods shed is on the left. The photographer is standing on the up platform, while the east end of the sharply-curved down platform is on the right. The signal box closed 22 February 1959 when a replacement was brought into use. Dr A.J.G.Dickens

4 **The Hamworthy Branch**

Birmingham
Railway Carriage
& Wagon Co 33
106 leaving
Hamworthy
Junction, 1 May
1986. The branch
to Hamworthy
Goods curves to the
left. Author

T HE HAMWORTHY branch was built as part of the Southampton &
Dorchester Railway. Hamworthy was the original station for both Poole
and Bournemouth. A lady visitor for Bournemouth arrived at Hamworthy
station and inquired how to reach Bournemouth. She was told by a porter that
although he had never been there, he knew that the best way to reach
Bournemouth was by Oxford. She thought this rather curious. The mystery was
solved when a horse bus arrived owned by G. Axford.

From 31 August 1863 daily trains ran through from Hamworthy to
Burnham-on-Sea giving a connecting service between the English and Bristol
Channels. In the summers of 1865 and 1866 the Somerset & Dorset Railway

Birmingham Railway Carriage & Wagon Co 33 106 leaving Hamworthy Junction, 1 May 1986. The branch to Hamworthy Goods curves to the left. Author

BR Standard Class 4 2-6-0 No 76015 at Hamworthy Goods on 14 July 1960. H.C. Casserley

Hamworthy Goods station 1965. J.H.Lucking

The delightful B4 class 0-4-0T No 92 at Hamworthy Goods station in 1947. C.T. Standfast

operated a steamer service from Hamworthy to Cherbourg, but the low number
of travellers made it uneconomic. The Hamworthy branch was doubled in 1863-
4 together with the rest of the Southampton and Dorchester, but traffic did not
warrant it and on 25 November 1905 it reverted to single track.

Lake Halt approximately midway along the branch opened during World
War One for J.R. Smith's shipyard workers, the siding being shunted by his own
locomotives. A siding also served the Admiralty Flying Boat Base. Although
Hamworthy closed to passengers as long ago as 1 July 1896, it still remains
open for freight.

The Railway
Enthusiasts' Club
special at
Hamworthy Goods
headed by M7 class
0-4-4T No 30107,
7 June 1958.
R.M.Casserley

0-6-0 diesel shunter
D2028 at
Hamworthy Goods
14 September 1966.
Paul Strong

Robert Stephenson & Hawthorn Co's Works No 7645 of 1949, *Western Pride* owned by Southern Wharves, at Hamworthy Goods, 30 September 1963. Revd Alan Newman

The 0-4-0 diesel shunter built by the Yorkshire Engine Co and owned by the Poole Harbour Commissioners, seen here at Hamworthy Quay, 16 August 1995. Author

5 Wimborne to Daggons Road

THE LINE BETWEEN West Moors and Daggons Road was part of a line from Alderbury Junction, four miles south of Salisbury, to join the Southampton & Dorchester, thus more than halving the distance between Salisbury and Poole compared with that via Eastleigh. Known as the Salisbury & Dorset Junction Railway, it received its Act on 22 July 1861. The contractors, Garrett & Co, began work on 3 February 1864 but payments to the company were slow, resulting him abandoning the contract which was then taken over by Henry Jackson. By October 1866 Jackson had run into financial difficulties so the railway company negotiated with the LSWR to complete the line.

It opened on 20 December 1866 and in due course, the LSWR which worked the line, handed over £14 to the Salisbury & Dorset Junction Railway as its share of income for the first six months. It was believed that a station at West

An M7 class 0-4-4T at Broadstone Junction propelling a passenger train towards Wimborne circa 1935.
Author's collection

West Country class Pacific No 34048 *Crediton* leaves Broadstone Junction with the 6.30pm Weymouth to Salisbury on August Bank Holiday Monday, 5 August 1963. R.A.Lumber

BR Standard Class 4 4-6-0 No 75065 approaches Broadstone Junction on August Bank Holiday Monday, 5 August 1963 with a Southampton Terminus to Bournemouth West train. The '20' sign indicates the speed limit. The 'barley sugar' lamp post deserves a second look. The sign 'SR Passengers must cross line by bridge' is supported on an old length of rail. R.A.Lumber

Moors would increase traffic and the station, which appeared like a row of terraced houses in an industrial street, opened on 1 August 1867, the Salisbury & Dorchester paying £20 annually towards its maintenance.

Fortunately receipts rose to £8,893 in 1875, but the line did not pay its way and so was sold to the LSWR on 31 October 1882. It flourished under the new ownership but was eventually identified by the 1963 Beeching Report as uneconomic so was closed completely on 4 May 1964, though latterly the line managed to fulfil the aims of its promoters and on Saturdays only, was used by a couple of expresses en route to Bournemouth, one from Wellington and the other from Llanelly.

The single platform at Daggons Road opened on 1 January 1876 as Alderholt, but was renamed on 1 May 1876 to avoid confusion with Aldershot. An unusual feature of the station was its nameboard attached to the booking

office roof. Verwood was a two-road station and from the goods yard, until about 1945 a private siding led to Verwood & Gotham Brick & Tile Company's works. Coal was received inwards and clay products were despatched. An unusual feature of the station was the fact that the Albion Hotel was actually situated within the station yard.

Wimborne 1963 showing the signal box unusually tall to offer good visibility. The 'barley sugar' lamp post supports a gas lamp. Lens of Sutton

West Moors circa 1905. The concrete footbridge was erected soon after 1900. Author's collection

A BR Standard tender engine at West Moors hauls auto set No 33 circa 1963. The signal is set for the Brockenhurst line, while the branch to Verwood and Salisbury curves left. Lens of Sutton

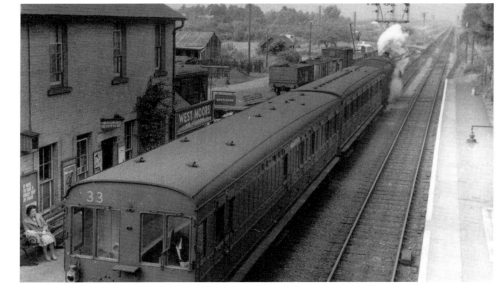

Verwood view up circa 1905. Notice the board-crossing for the station staff. The signal box is on the left. Author's collection

A down passenger train headed by Adams 460 class 4-4-0 No 467 enters the single platform Daggons Road station circa 1910. Unusually the name board is set on the station roof. Author's collection

6 Wareham to Swanage

LSWR poster of circa 1910 advertising Swanage. Author's collection

THE SWANAGE RAILWAY ACT received Royal Assent on 18 July 1881. The tender of Curry & Reeves was accepted and work began on 5 June 1883. The bridges constructed between Corfe and Swanage were built to allow for the track to be doubled as it was expected that traffic would develop to such an extent that the line would need doubling. The stations at Corfe and Swanage were constructed of Purbeck stone by Bull & Company of Southampton. The line opened to passengers and parcels on 20 May 1885, the 22 minute journey from Wareham comparing very favourably with the one and a half hours taken by the horse bus. It was normal practice for branch lines to be worked by old engines, but the first locomotive on the Swanage line was Adams 4-4-2T No 67 sent new from Robert Stephenson's works. Goods traffic commenced on 1 June 1885.

The railway affected Swanage as good transport enabled it to develop as a fashionable resort, while commercially, all Purbeck stone could now be removed by rail and shipping was no longer used. This was fortunate as only vessels of 300 tons or less could enter the bay and ships of this size were not really economic. In 1886 the LSWR took over the Swanage Railway.

The branch was dieselised on 5 September 1966 and paid its way until January 1968 when a different method of accounting placed it in the red. Closure was considered but after hearing evidence that buses would be unable to handle summer traffic, the Department of the Environment inspector decided that the line should stay open, but was over-ruled by the Secretary of the Department of the Environment. Passenger traffic ceased on 3 January 1972 and the track east of Furzebrook lifted. Worgret Junction to Furzebrook was retained for clay traffic and the development of the Wytch Farm oilfield led to the opening of a tank wagon terminal on 12 December 1978. When in 1989-90 a pipeline carried oil to Hamble refinery, the terminal was converted to handling butane and propane gas.

M7 class 0-4-4T No 30052 near Worgret Junction propelling the 4.57 pm Wareham to Swanage 4 May 1963. Author

Furzebrook oil terminal, 1 May 1986, view down, with the English Clays siding on the right. Author

Norden, view down, 16 August 1995. Notice the Corfe Castle fixed distant signal. The bridge formerly carried Fayle's Tramway. (See page 154) Author

'Hampshire' diesel-electric multiple-unit No 1127 calls at Corfe Castle en route from Swanage to Wareham 12 October 1971. R.A.Lumber

Ex-GWR '57XX' class 0-6-0PT No 7714 leaves Corfe Castle for Norden 10 November 2007. K.Hampton

Leaving the main line at Worgret Junction, the branch crossed the River Frome by viaducts of six and three spans respectively, each span being of 34ft; they were constructed by E.G.Perkins of Lymington. East of Furzebrook Sidings, two more sidings were opened on 18 November 1940 for two mobile guns and two locomotives manned by military personnel. These sidings were taken out of use in the summer of 1946. At Eldon Siding, renamed Norden Siding in September 1950, clay was transferred from narrow gauge to standard gauge wagons. This siding closed on 22 March 1966. Just before Corfe Castle station the line crosses a four-arch stone viaduct. The bridges between Worgret Junction and Corfe are of stone, while those beyond are of brick. Swanage station was sensitively altered in 1937 in order to cope with the increased traffic. Its water supply came from a deep well and was raised by a steam pump driven from the train heating pipe of the branch locomotive. When the pump was taken away for

Battle of Britain class Pacific No 34072 *257 Squadron* at Harman's Cross working the 13.00 Swanage to Norden 16 August 1995. The concrete permanent way cabin on the far right was designed so that it could be carried on a railway wagon without fouling the gauge. Author

repair, water was brought in old locomotive tenders.

Some trains ran through from Waterloo headed by tender engines which had to return tender-first as they were too long for the 50ft diameter turntable at Swanage. Sometimes through specials from the S&D or GWR brought 'foreign' locomotives to Swanage. On 11 & 12 February 1944 special trains carried Prime Minister Winston Churchill, King George VI, the Allied Commander General Eisenhower and General Montgomery to Swanage to watch D-Day landing rehearsals at Studland Bay. General Eisenhower had a cinema coach in his train.

Closure of most of the branch in 1972 was far from being the end of the story. Unfortunately BR lifted the track before the preservation society had a chance to raise funds for its purchase. Swanage station was bought by the local council and leased to the preservation society. Track was relaid and the line gradually reached Herston Halt, Harman's Cross, Corfe Castle and eventually Norden was attained on 12 August 1995. The latter is a park and ride station, the idea proving to be a winner as it allows tourists to avoid parking problems at Swanage and as a bonus enjoy a delightful train journey through the Purbeck countryside. At the time of writing the Swanage Railway hopes to run through trains to Wareham.

From the later nineteen-twenties, one particularly interesting feature of the branch was the working of local passenger trains. In order to avoid the time and trouble to signalman and footplate staff at each terminus uncoupling, running round the train and recoupling, push-pull working was instituted. This meant that the engine stayed at one end of the train and when returning, the driver controlled the engine from a special vestibule at the end of the coach in what had become the leading end of the train. The locomotive's regulator was remotely operated by compressed air. An engine normally pushed its train from Wareham to Swanage and drew it in the reverse direction.

'Hampshire' diesel-electric multiple-unit No 1125 north of Swanage with the 14.35 Swanage to Wareham, 15 April 1967. Author

M7 class 0-4-4T
No 30057 on the
turntable outside
Swanage
locomotive shed
circa 1950.
Author's collection

Preservationists have relaid track and turntable and this scene, on 1 May 1986, was as it had been 36 years earlier. The locomotive is M7 class 0-4-4T No 30053. Author

When the M7 class locomotives were withdrawn, they were replaced by LMS-designed Class 2 2-6-2Ts. Here No 41303 passes Swanage engine shed and takes the crossover to the bay platform circa 1965. David Lawrence

Swanage station at its opening, 20 May 1885. Author's collection

An early view, circa 1887, of a passenger train at Swanage headed by 2-4-0WT No 209. Notice the 'Birdcage' brake vans designed to offer guards a good lookout. A van stands in the bay platform. Author's collection

M7 class 0-4-4T No 30128 has just arrived at Swanage propelling a train from Wareham circa 1959. The red tail lamp is still placed to the left of the headcode disc. Coaches for a through working to Waterloo stand in the bay platform, right. Author's collection

View towards the buffers at Swanage circa 1959. M7 class 0-4-4T No 30128 heads a train to Wareham. Notice the corridor coaches in the goods yard. These were required for through trains to Waterloo. The signal box is designed to give plenty of light to the interior. Author's collection

The attractive exterior of Swanage station, 16 August 1995. Author

7 **Weymouth to Portland & Easton**

THE WEYMOUTH & Portland Railway Act received Royal Assent on 30 June 1862 and by an agreement of 18 March 1862 the line was to be worked jointly by the GWR and LSWR. John Aird & Son won the building contract on 30 July 1862. Navvies were well-known for causing trouble. Mr Fairey, a Weymouth boot and shoe dealer, was tricked by a navvy who asked to try on a pair of boots. He said that they seemed to fit, but to make sure, would try and dance in them. He capered towards the door and then ran out without paying.

Soon after, another navvy, giving the impression of being a ganger, went into a beer house on the Island of Portland to see if there was a room sufficiently large to pay the men in. A few days later he complained that it was too small. The owner then took him upstairs to a room which he said was 'Just the thing'. The navvy then cautioned the proprietor not to trust any of the other navvies who came unless he was with them, then ordered a quantity of beer which one

A general view of Portland station circa 1923. The goods and stone works are straight ahead; several cranes are available for loading and unloading. The passenger station and line to Easton are on the left. Author's collection

O2 class 0-4-4T No 207 at Portland circa 1920. Author's collection

O2 class 0-4-4T No 30230 leaving Portland station circa 1950. Author's collection

of his men collected. This was repeated many times a day during the week. One of the leading men employed by the contractor, when in conversation with the publican remarked that the man who had rented the room was not a ganger, but an ordinary navvy. An inquiry was started, the navvy's suspicions were aroused and he made his escape with the proceeds of the sale of beer to his workmates. The only thing the landlord got out of it was the nickname 'Ganger Jack'.

The opening of the Weymouth & Portland Railway on 16 October 1865 offered an alternative form of transport for Portland stone as transfer sidings were laid at Castleton for the transhipment of stone from one railway to another. Transhipment was necessary because the Portland Railway's relatively light wagons were unsuited for main line running and the gauge was 4ft 6in instead of 4ft 8½in or 7ft 0¼in. Transhipment was aided by an overhead gantry crane spanning the tracks of both railways.

The Weymouth & Portland was leased in perpetuity to the GWR and LSWR and built to accommodate broad gauge GWR trains as well as those of the standard gauge LSWR. In actual fact, as the original passenger service was worked by the LSWR, GWR freight trains were the only ones to use the broad gauge rails.

In 1867 a quite separate 1½ mile long broad gauge line was begun, built for the purpose of transporting stone from Easton to Church Hope Cove, but only two thirds of a mile was constructed before Parliamentary powers expired in 1872.

The next proposal was the 'Admiralty' line whereby the GWR and LSWR provided rail access to the Admiralty breakwater, principally for the use of coal

The dramatic result of a landslip near Easton, November 1907. Author's collection

Easton station caught fire on 28 November 1903 – it had opened on 1 September 1902. The line to the engine shed had yet to be built. The line on the left led to Sheepcroft stone sidings. Author's collection

traffic for fuelling the fleet. Completed in 1877 and opened the following year, it was just over a mile in length and most of the wagons were drawn by horses.

In 1883 plans were put forward for extending the unfinished Easton & Church Hope Cove line and converting it to standard gauge to join the Weymouth & Portland Railway with running powers over the Admiralty line. Strict clauses in the Act of Parliament prevented the line from obstructing Admiralty land and rifle ranges, or making it easier for convicts to escape from the prison work yard. In due course to avoid causing trouble the gunners were provided with a railway timetable and engine drivers were ordered to watch for red flags.

Construction of the line did not begin until 1888 and it took no less than twelve years for the 3½ miles of railway to be built, (much of it through solid rock), to link with the Admiralty line. McNay was appointed the company's engineer in 1885 and in 1897 he rebelled over his unpaid account by confiscating plans and working drawings and thus preventing them being signed by the railway contractor. He was instantly dismissed and replaced by Messrs Packman, Popkiss & Heasman.

O2 class 0-4-4T No 212 at Easton with a train to Weymouth circa 1934. At least four of the coaches have trellis gates rather than doors. Author's collection

The cramped situation of Easton station is obvious in this view. The four coaches are headed by an O2 class 0-4-4T. Author's collection

Worked jointly by the GWR and the LSWR, the line was opened to Easton on 1 October 1900. Unfortunately the Board of Trade inspector would not allow passenger traffic to start until the Admiralty line had been brought up to standard, but much to the chagrin of the Easton & Church Hope Company, it was still required to pay the charge of £900 for using the Admiralty line – the rental including the operation of passenger trains which it was not allowed to run.

In 1900 the Admiralty terminated its agreement with the GWR and the LSWR. This allowed the Easton & Church Hope to secure the Admiralty line and carry out the necessary improvements. The line to Easton was eventually opened for passenger traffic on 1 September 1902. On this date a new station was opened at Portland on the curve to Easton, the former terminal station there being relegated to a goods depot. Although from 1 September 1902 the Portland & Easton lines were worked as one branch, the Weymouth & Portland and Easton & Church Hope companies (the latter in Receivership since 1901) retained their nominal independence until Nationalisation in 1948.

'57XX' class 0-6-0PT No 4624 stands at Easton 8 July 1956 with the Railway Correspondence & Travel Society's 'The Wessex Wyvern'. R.A.Lumber

The picturesque 3½ mile long line wormed its way round the fort of the Verne and hugged the east coast. The single track ran on a ledge between the perpendicular cliff and the sea, following each curve of the coastline and rising sharply all the time. To avoid a train being derailed by a rock fall, a 211yd long wire screen was erected so that in the event of a stone fall breaking a wire, signals were automatically thrown to danger and a bell rung in both Easton and Portland signal boxes. When the line reached the centre of the island, it turned sharply inland through a narrow cutting blasted out of solid rock and terminated at the single platform station at Easton, surrounded by quarries.

The line being paralleled by a main road was susceptible to bus competition and this, coupled with the fact that the isle's population had declined, caused the regular passenger train service to be withdrawn on 3 March 1952, the engine shed at Easton closing on the same date. From 1940 until 1944 Easton had been served by passenger trains only during the summer months. During World War Two the branch was blocked 13 times by enemy action and the Easton section cut off for several months. The line from Weymouth to Easton was closed completely on 5 April 1965.

The entrance to Easton, 15 September 1957. On the left is a ground frame hut. R.A.Lumber

A particularly interesting station on the branch was that at Melcombe Regis. As Weymouth station was a terminus, it meant that a train to Portland had to reverse after leaving in order to reach the branch. To avoid the time-consuming procedure of uncoupling the engine from its coaches and running round the train, on 30 May 1909 Melcombe Regis station was opened actually on the branch, but adjacent to the main station, though the GWR still ran a through coach for eight or more prisoners travelling to Portland. As Melcombe Regis was exposed to the prevailing south westerly winds, a large screen was erected which blocked views of the Backwater, but made life pleasanter in inclement weather. Although closed to regular traffic on 3 May 1952 when the branch closed to passengers, until 12 September 1959 it was opened on Saturdays to relieve traffic from the main line platforms, or when congestion was experienced at Weymouth Quay, or the quay tramway was flooded.

On 18 December 1899 Fireman Frank Willis was on the footplate of the locomotive hauling the 6.50pm to Portland. At first he was busy attending to the fire, but then he looked away from it in order to accustom his eyes to the darkness the better to spot signals at Rodwell. Wondering why they were travelling so slowly, he was about to ask Percy Nutman his driver, but was alarmed to see him missing. He stopped the train, the line was searched, but no trace of the body could be found. Next day his cap was found on Backwater Viaduct, the inference being that he had fallen into the creek and drowned. For three days the Backwater was dragged, but no body recovered.

Early in January 1900 his wife offered a reward of £25 for the recovery of his corpse. The railway police investigated and discovered that Percy Nutman was in fact living at Fetcham, near Leatherhead with his wife's younger sister who was expecting his child. There he was working as a woodcutter. He was arrested and stood trial at Dorchester Quarter Sessions in July 1900 charged with 'unlawfully and wilfully leaving an engine whereby the lives and persons

Melcombe Regis station facing the Backwater, the steel viaduct is on the right. Author's collection

Melcombe Regis station shortly after its opening on 30 May 1909. When travelling bunker-first, the footplate crew on this engine lacked shelter in inclement weather. Author's collection

of those travelling along the Great Western and South Western Portland Joint Railway might have been endangered'. He was given six months' hard labour in Dorchester Gaol.

The Portland Joint Railway uniform was provided by the GWR and was similar to its own uniform but lettered 'W&PR'. Staff vacancies were filled alternately by the GWR and LSWR. When the Fleet was in at Portland, the last train from Weymouth in the evening was sometimes so crowded that if the guard was a weak character, he let them hang on the outside of the coaches, sometimes still swigging beer.

Portland station was low-lying and when a high tide and west wind coincided the station became flooded. If the water was 3ft deep trains stopped until the tide went out.

O2 class No 227 at
Melcombe Regis,
11 October 1931.
The end of the
windscreen can be
seen on the left.
H.C.Casserley

The Backwater at Weymouth was originally crossed by a timber trestle bridge with 66 openings. This was replaced 1907-9 with a steel viaduct. Part of the Backwater was filled with chalk from widening a cutting at Dorchester Junction. In 1897 the Weymouth stationmaster was reprimanded for allowing three engines to cross the viaduct with a Paddington to Portland excursion as their combined weight hazarded the structure.

Immediately north of Rodwell station was a 58yd long tunnel. When Rodwell cutting was excavated Roman pottery and coins were found.

The Fleet Viaduct had 27 timber spans but in 1903 was replaced by an iron bridge of 6 spans laid parallel to the original structure. In 1940 decking was laid flush with the rails. Why? So that in an emergency, perhaps caused by enemy raiders, it could be used by road vehicles. Railway and road ran parallel for ¾ mile along the Chesil Beach and a six foot high wall erected to prevent locomotives alarming horses. Although the Easton line was worked by the GWR and the LSWR, (later by the SR), it remained an independent company until Nationalisation in 1948.

0-6-0ST No 2086 crosses the timber viaduct at Melcombe Regis circa 1905. Notice that the gradient rises from right to left. Author's collection

LSWR C14 class 2-2-0T No 742 approaches Wyke Regis Halt circa 1910 hauling a motor train set with trellis gates instead of doors. Author's collection

Rodwell station, view up circa 1905 towards the 58yd long Rodwell Tunnel. Author's collection

The derelict-looking goods yard, Portland, 22 July 1966. Author

8 Gillingham to Yeovil

THE SALISBURY & Yeovil Railway Bill had a close escape from rejection. The official responsible for advertising the Bill in a certain newspaper neglected to do so until the date required by Standing Orders had expired. The difficulty was cunningly surmounted by arranging with the journal's manager to print some copies of the issue containing the advertisement with an altered date, and those fraudulent copies were produced to the Examiner of Private Bills. That official, having been warned of the deception, reported the matter to the House of Commons, at the same time certifying that Standing Orders had not been complied with. The newspaper manager was summoned to attend and explain his conduct, and confessed his delinquency. To everyone's surprise, the House resolved that the Standing Orders should be dispensed with.

50 027 *Lion* enters Gillingham with the 06.43 Exeter to Waterloo 21 June 1986. There is a good crowd of passengers. Author

Warship class diesel-hydraulic *Highflyer* near Buckhorn Weston tunnel with a train from Brighton, 4 August 1964. This was one of the earliest appearances of a Warship on this line. Author

The first sod was cut at Gillingham on 3 April 1856. Rain soaked through the canvas of the marquee and dripped into guests' glasses which caused one wit to remark, 'We've had so much cold water thrown on us by this project, that a bucket or two extra can make no difference'. One newspaper reporting the event wrote: 'If continuous rain throughout the day be an indication of success, this undertaking will have more than its fair share.' On the date of this ceremony the railway had only £4 5s 0d in its bank account – rather a small sum to begin construction of a line which was to cost over £½m but eventually paid its shareholders a dividend of 12½%. That high figure was achieved partly because

West Country class Pacific No 34036 *Westward Ho!* on a rising gradient of 1 in 100, heading a down freight approaching Buckhorn Weston Tunnel, 4 August 1964. Towards the front of the train are empty ballast wagons bound for Meldon Quarry. This engine was probably unique in having an exclamation mark in its name. Author

BR Standard Class
4 2-6-0 No 76067
approaching
Buckhorn Weston
Tunnel with the
11.10 am Salisbury
to Exeter, 4 August
1964. Author

BR Standard Class 4 2-6-0 No 76067 approaching Buckhorn Weston Tunnel with the 11.10 am Salisbury to Exeter, 4 August 1964. Author

Sir William Tite, architect to the LSWR. Author's collection

of an attractive working arrangement and partly because the directors, unlike those of some other railways, avoided building feeder branches which often proved to be only expensive suckers.

The line was opened between Salisbury and Gillingham on 2 May 1859, but the major work between Salisbury and Yeovil was the 742yd long Buckhorn Weston Tunnel, water from the greensand causing problems. Additional shafts were sunk to improve drainage and allowed the excavation to progress at 12 faces. The tunnel was completed on 17 February 1860, and Shaft No 3 left open for ventilation. The extension to Sherborne was opened 7 May 1860.

The line opened to Yeovil on 1 June 1860, trains terminating at the Bristol & Exeter's Hendford station. The Board of Trade was unhappy with engines working tender-first and had insisted on a temporary turntable at Gillingham when that station was a terminus, and similarly at Sherborne. It was actually the same turntable which had been moved down the line. At Hendford a problem arose in converting the broad gauge turntable to mixed gauge, so the LSWR arranged for the Sherborne turntable to be moved to Yeovil.

To complete the story, on 18 July 1860 the line was extended to Exeter, and a joint GWR and LSWR station opened at Yeovil Town on 1 June 1861.

Traffic developed to such an extent that the line was doubled later in the eighteen-sixties. In places insufficient room had been left for doubling and clearance was tight. Captain Tyler inspecting the line for the Board of Trade twice rejected the second line between Gillingham and Templecombe, and only after the Salisbury & Yeovil directors personally visited the Board was the second track

Sherborne station view up circa 1910. On the left are milk churns, newspaper posters leaning against the iron fence and shutters to block the front of W.H.Smith & Sons' bookstall when closed. Author's collection

A line of porters' trolleys at Sherborne circa 1965. Author's collection

DMU 159 001 At Yeovil Junction working the 08.35 Waterloo to Paignton, 6 September 1999. Author

Diesel-hydraulic Warship class No 822 *Hercules* leaves Yeovil Junction with the 10.20 Exeter St David's to Waterloo, 3 October 1971, the last day that locomotives of this class worked the route. It is crossing the Yeovil (Pen Mill) to Dorchester line and on the right, above *Hercules*, can be seen the line to Yeovil Town. R.A.Lumber

Yeovil Junction view down circa 1910. Author's collection

Yeovil Junction view down, 4 April 1989. The down island platform, left, has been taken out of public use. Author

S15 class 4-6-0 No 30831 at Yeovil Junction, 14 August 1960, heads the 12.00 noon to Salisbury. Edwin Wilmshurst

allowed to be opened. Permission was granted subject to the working company, the LSWR, undertaking to place notices in its coaches warning passengers not to put their heads out of the windows, or open the doors of a moving train. This was done because the LSWR had absolutely refused to place bars across the windows which would have created a prison cell atmosphere. The Salisbury & Yeovil Railway was taken over by the LSWR in 1877.

The first LSWR station in Dorset was Gillingham. The station building was designed by the LSWR's architect Sir William Tite, MP for Bath. One of his features was slate-hung walls to keep out the damp. Early in the twentieth century the station nameboard read:'Gillingham for Mere', the LSWR subscribing for a two-horse bus to serve the village.

Yeovil Junction station was just in Dorset. It originally consisted of two island platforms joined by a roof. The track design was poor as curves caused non-stop trains to be restricted to 20mph. In 1929 the station was re-modelled with the through non-stop lines completely straight. Sherborne was the only other station on the line in Dorset, the building being another of Tite's creations.

It is a little-known fact that the LSWR planned to have a water trough straddling the Dorset-Somerset border just east of Templecombe. Unlike most other large railway companies, the South Western did not have troughs between the rails in order that locomotives could replenish their water without stopping. In 1907 Dugald Drummond, its locomotive engineer, planned a class of engine which he believed could run non-stop from London to Exeter without the need to change engines at Salisbury. The tender of this new engine was actually built with water pick-up apparatus, but the engine proved useless, the scheme was abandoned and the pick-up apparatus removed. Although many of the stations between Exeter and Salisbury were closed on 7 March 1966 and much of the line singled the following year, the three stations in Dorset remain open.

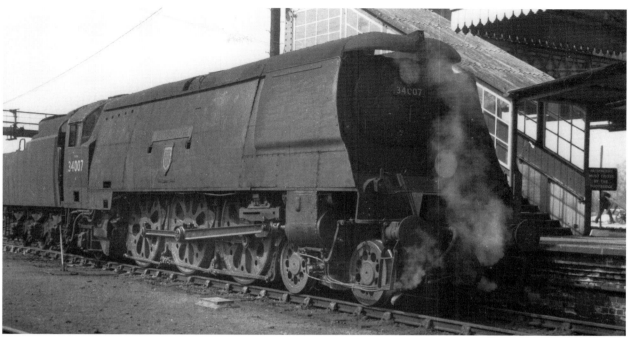

West Country Pacific No 34007 *Wadebridge* at Yeovil Junction, 2 April 1965. Revd Alan Newman

Diesel-hydraulic Warship class D831 *Monarch* shunting milk tanks at Yeovil Junction, 15 April 1967. Author

T9 class 4-4-0 No 122 at Yeovil Junction circa 1910. LSWR engines generally had extra large tenders, dubbed 'water carts', as, unlike most other railways, they had no water troughs to allow an engine to pick up water while moving. Author's collection

The turntable at Yeovil Junction, 4 April 1989, with the passenger station in the background. Author

9 Other LSWR Branches

Poole Quay and West Bay Branches

Parliamentary powers for building a branch to Poole Quay were included in the Poole and Bournemouth Railway Act of 26 May 1865. Built by the contractor Charles Waring, it opened with the Bournemouth & Poole line on 15 June 1874. It was worked by the LSWR and absorbed by that company in 1883. Initially horse-worked, steam took over in 1899. As the line ran along public roads speed was restricted to 4mph and an engine was preceded by a man carrying red and green flags during the day, or red and green lights after dark. The last train on

Lyme Regis circa 1908. Author's collection

Ex-LBSCR 'Terrier'
tank engine as
LSWR No 735 at
Lyme Regis August
1903. Notice the
flat-bottomed
track. Author's
collection

the line ran on 30 April 1960. Running parallel with the tramway were the West Bay Military Sidings laid circa 1915 and lifted in January 1920.

Holton Heath Cordite Factory Branch

This branch diverged from the up line east of Holton Heath station to serve a cordite factory opened circa 1914. The various scattered buildings were served by standard gauge lines. At the far end of the layout, the line continued for ½ mile before crossing the main line and serving Rockley Jetty in Wareham Channel. The factory closed circa 1961 and the railway subsequently dismantled.

The line was worked by Royal Naval Cordite Factory locomotives. A 2ft 6in gauge system to the north of the complex was worked by two fireless steam engines which received steam from a stationary boiler. It was also worked by petrol-mechanical, diesel-mechanical and battery-electric locomotives.

Axminster to Lyme Regis

Most of the Axminster to Lyme Regis branch was in Devon, only crossing into Dorset prior to passing below the A3070 about ½ mile before the terminus at Lyme Regis.

The Axminster & Lyme Regis Light Railway obtained its Light Railway Order on 15 June 1899, a 'light railway' being a line which, subject to certain restrictions such as being worked at a lower speed, could be built and worked more cheaply. Arthur C. Pain, appointed as the line's engineer, was almost the Father of Light Railways and in 1872 engineered the Culm Valley Railway in Devon. Pain had excellent credentials having been trained by Brunel's chief assistant R.P.Brereton. On 10 April 1900 Baldry & Yerburgh's tender for building the line was signed and all shares taken by 5 July 1900.

A 'Terrier' tank engine at Lyme Regis in October 1903 with a train consisting of a van and four passenger coaches. The goods shed is in its original position. Author's collection

Lyme Regis in the 'thirties showing the goods shed in its new position. Author's collection

4-4-2T No 3520 at
Lyme Regis in the
'thirties. Author's
collection

To enable the line to be constructed as cheaply as possible, it followed a
sinuous course, the major engineering feature being Cannington Viaduct 203yd
in length composed of ten arches. The structure was built of concrete, an aerial
ropeway carrying the material to where is was required. In February 1902 frost
caused work to be stopped for 14 days, while another problem developed when
the contractors' locomotive being hauled to the site, jammed between the two
banks of a narrow lane near Trill.

Anticipating opening on 1 June, the Board of Trade inspection was fixed for
18 May 1903, but this notice had to be withdrawn when heavy rain caused

4-4-2T No 3125 At Lyme Regis in the 'thirties. Author's collection

a serious subsidence at the western end of the viaduct. To strengthen it, two arches, one above the other, were built within arch No 3. As the railway could not be used from 1 June, the LSWR arranged for a horse omnibus to make trips between Lyme and Axminster connecting with mainline trains. This bus took 50 minutes in each direction, fares being two shillings inside and one shilling and sixpence outside. Through third class tickets were issued from Lyme to London and vice versa for 13 shillings. The work of strengthening the viaduct proceeded quickly and the first train ran on 24 August 1903; one train having no less than 13 coaches, was hauled by two engines. All were subject to a limit of 15 mph over the viaduct.

The LSWR which had worked the line from the beginning, took over the local company on 1 January 1907. The following year it is recorded that 60,000 passengers, 1,900 parcels and 8,000 tons of goods travelled over the line, particularly heavy traffic being experienced that year, as from January to June sightseers came to view the burning cliff.

As it was built as a light railway, no signals were erected, so telephones were used to warn stations when a train had left. An overall speed limit of 25mph was enforced, with a lower limit to 10mph around curves of less than 9 chains radius. The LSWR installed signals in July 1906, but the wheel turned full circle when on 27 March 1960 'one train working' was introduced by BR, all signals being removed.

Lyme Regis in the nineteen-thirties. W.H. Smith's bookstall is on the platform. A corridor coach for a through train to Waterloo stands on the right. Author's collection

4-4-2T No 30583 of 72A, Exmouth Junction shed, at Lyme Regis circa 1955 with coach set No 44. Author's collection

The hand-operated yard crane at Lyme Regis circa 1954. A.E.West

Ex-LMS Class 2 2-6-2T No 41297 on trial at Lyme Regis, 18 September 1960. A.E.West

Single car DMU W55000 at Lyme Regis, 14 May 1964. A.E. West

Although busy on summer Saturdays, road transport took traffic from the railway and by 1952 the average number of passengers on a train worked out at 2½ in winter and 7 in summer. Final trains ran on 29 November 1965 and as stocks of Lyme Regis to Axminster day returns were exhausted, adults were issued with two children's tickets.

Lyme Regis station was set 249ft above sea level and half a mile from the sea, the timber building having an almost flat roof, but later given one with a steeper pitch. The building may still be seen today at Alresford on the Mid Hants Railway.

On 28 December 1912 there was excitement when the timber-built engine shed at Lyme Regis ignited, but fortunately the engine was removed before it became damaged. Learning from the experience, the second shed was built of asbestos on steel framing.

The opening of the branch posed a problem for Dugald Drummond, the LSWR locomotive engineer. The company's existing engines were thought to be unsuitable for the 9 chain radius curves and not within the weight restrictions. He contemplated building two special engines, but then decided on the cheaper solution of buying two second-hand 'Terrier' 0-6-0 tank engines from the London, Brighton & South Coast Railway. They proved to be insufficiently powerful for the heavy summer traffic and suffered from excessive tyre wear. One of these engines was sold to the Freshwater, Yarmouth & Newport Railway on the Isle of Wight, later returning to the mainland to work the Hayling Island service. Restored as LBSCR *Newington* in 1966 she was placed outside the inn 'The Hayling Billy' as an outsize pub sign. In 1979 the brewers, Whitbread Wessex, donated her to the Wight Locomotive Society.

The 'Terriers' were replaced on the Lyme Regis branch by standard '02' class

Ex-GWR 0-4-2T No 1462 arriving at Lyme Regis 12 November 1958 with the 11.00 am ex Axminster. Collection P.K.Tunks

0-4-4 tank engines which were made sufficiently light by the tanks and bunker being only partly filled. The '02s' were not a roaring success as they suffered from excessive flange wear and distorted frames. Eventually an Adams' '415' class 4-4-2 tank engine was tried with specially modified bogie to give greater side play and thereby ease the negotiation of severe curves in which the branch abounded. For almost 50 years this class had a monopoly of the branch. In 1946, both engines, now the sole survivors of this class on the Southern Railway, needed heavy repairs. There was but one other engine of this class still extant, a locomotive sold by the LSWR to the Government General Salvage Depot at Sittingbourne in 1917 and bought by the East Kent Railway two years later. Although it had lain derelict since 1939 it was in repairable condition, was overhauled and put into SR service. Following extensive track renewals and re-aligning of curves in 1960, it was possible to use more modern locomotives and the Adams' tanks were withdrawn, but fortunately the Bluebell Railway preserved No 30583 – the one rescued from the East Kent Railway

Yeovil Junction to Yeovil Town Branch

As the main LSWR station, Yeovil Junction, was 1¾ miles from the town itself, a frequent shuttle service was operated between Yeovil Junction and Yeovil Town, the branch being one of the shortest in the country. As explained on page 72, Yeovil Junction had two island platforms, the outer faces were used by through trains and the single centre road for shuttle trains to and from Yeovil Town station, the layout allowing passengers to transfer to or from any main line train simply by crossing a platform. When the layout was modified in 1909 the loop on the up side was used for Yeovil Town trains.

Curving northwards from Yeovil Junction the line ran alongside the Wilts, Somerset & Weymouth Railway, but although parallel, it was not until World War Two that Yeovil South Junction was opened on 13 October 1943 at the point where the lines diverged. Canadian troops laid this connection in the remarkable time of three days. Beyond the junction the line crossed the 62yd long River Yeo Viaduct and passed into Somerset. Both routes were singled on 26 May 1968 and the line beyond to Yeovil Town closed on 1 March 1967.

In its early days the branch was worked by small tank engines, but in 1903 ex-LBSCR 'Terrier' 0-6-0T No 646 *Newington*, which had become LSWR No 734, worked trains. It had been purchased to work the Lyme Regis branch and was put to work at Yeovil while work on constructing the Lyme Regis branch was completed. Push and pull trains were introduced in July 1915 using a wire and pulley system to control the regulator, but in the late twenties this was replaced by the more efficient compressed air operation. As the line was allocated to the Western Region of BR in March 1963 ex-GWR engines appeared on the shuttle, replacing those of the SR. Following the closure of the Cirencester and Tetbury branches, from 28 December 1964 two of the four railbuses used on these service were utilised on the Junction to Town shuttle. Shorter than a conventional diesel railcar, they ran on four rather than eight wheels, seating 46 passengers with space for luggage.

The view circa 1908 from the west end of Yeovil Junction: a Yeovil Town branch passenger train can be seen below the footbridge. Author's collection

O2 class 0-4-4T No 30182 at Yeovil Junction with the shuttle service to Yeovil Town. The compressed air apparatus for working the regulator can be seen beside the smokebox. Revd Alan Newman

M7 class 0-4-4T No 30046 leaves Yeovil Junction for Yeovil Town 30 October 1954. On the right is Merchant Navy class Pacific No 35013 *Blue Funnel*. It is interesting comparing the locomotive sizes. Revd Alan Newman

Ex-GWR 54XX class 0-6-0PT No 5410 on the auto service from Yeovil Town, 13 April 1963. R.A.Lumber

Railbus W79975 approaches Yeovil Junction from Yeovil Town, 2 April 1965. Revd Alan Newman

On 9 August 1964 West Country class Pacific No 34108 *Wincanton* arrives at Yeovil Junction with the 15.50 to Salisbury. When it runs round the train it will face the right way. R.A. Lumber

Railbus W79975 at Yeovil Junction 1966, having worked from Yeovil Town. D. Payne

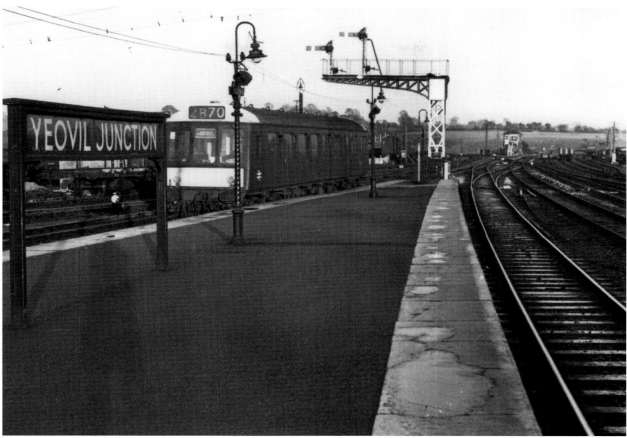

Single car DMU W55023 arrives at Yeovil Junction from Yeovil (Pen Mill), 16 December 1967. The photographer's shadow can be seen on the platform. R.A. Lumber

The 9.30am Exeter Central to Weymouth excursion traverses Yeovil South Junction on Sunday 3 August 1958, the signal box having to be opened specially for this working. The engine is Battle of Britain class Pacific No 34060 *25 Squadron*. R.A.Lumber

10 The Great Western Railway Group

An up train from
Weymouth passing
below the Salisbury
to Yeovil line, 14
June 1988. Author

The Wilts, Somerset & Weymouth Railway

The Wilts, Somerset and Weymouth Railway originally began as a line to serve
parts of Wiltshire and Somerset south of the GWR's London to Bristol line only
going as far as Yeovil where it was to join the Bristol & Exeter's Durston (near
Taunton) to Yeovil, Dorchester and Weymouth line. The GWR and the B&E
later decided it would be better if the WSWR was extended to Weymouth and
the B&E line cut short at Yeovil.

Thornford Bridge Halt, view up, 5 April 1966. Author

Yetminster, view down circa 1962. Lens of Sutton

DMUs W51576/90 plus intermediate trailer at Chetnole Halt with the 09.40 Bristol (Temple Meads) to Weymouth, 15 February 1973.

The south portal of Evershot Tunnel, 4 August 1981. Author

The up platform, Evershot, 1906. The building is of timber. Collection D. Score

On 30 November 1844 a public meeting at Weymouth supported the WSWR and in due course the necessary Act of Parliament was passed on 30 June 1845, the year of the Railway Mania and in its aftermath with so many lines in the country being built, there was a serious shortage of surveyors and draughtsmen and a start on the line was delayed. By February 1846 shafts had been sunk for Evershot Tunnel but in the winter of 1846-7, water percolating through the greensand caused problems. A start on the Dorchester to Weymouth section was delayed as Bincombe Tunnel was on a deviation and this was not sanctioned by Parliament until 25 June 1847.

This delay was frustrating to the inhabitants of Weymouth, seriously worried as the opening of the London & Southampton line had caused the Channel Island packets which had hitherto sailed from Weymouth, being transferred to Southampton on 26 May 1845. In August 1846 Brunel arranged with Messrs Dodson & Munday of Weymouth to carry out the Dorchester to Weymouth contract for £112,000 within 22 months and made a similar agreement with George Wythes of Brighton for the Dorchester to Maiden Newton contract at £95,000. Unfortunately the Railway Mania caused people to speculate and make an initial payment for shares and then be quite incapable of paying further calls for cash when a contractor required payment for work done.

Although the Southampton & Dorchester, which also received its Act in 1845, managed to open in 1847, the construction of the WSWR was much more tardy and by 1848 the line had only reached Westbury. It was thought that matters could be improved if efforts were concentrated into opening the section from Westbury to Frome, so on 4 June 1849 the GWR secretary sent a letter to the directors of the associated WSWR that it was the 'strong and decided' opinion of his directors that all other work should cease. George Wythes at work on the Dorchester to Maiden Newton section claimed compensation for this delay. By that August the short tunnels at Frampton and Evershot were finished apart from the portals. The only principal works remaining were the short tunnel at Poundbury and the nearby viaduct and bridge.

Navvies terrorised the countryside. One navvy was killed at Maiden Newton and after his funeral, navvies attacked people connected with the White Horse Inn and smashed all its windows.

A mishap occurred in January 1857. Between Bincombe Tunnel and Weymouth the chain linking the contractor's spoil wagons snapped causing them to run down the gradient completely out of control, the brakesman having leapt out to avoid the impending catastrophe. On entering Weymouth station they derailed and piled up, the noise being heard from almost a mile away.

The Dorchester to Weymouth section was mixed gauge so that the GWR broad gauge trains and those of the standard gauge LSWR could both be accommodated. The line opened to Weymouth on 20 January 1857, but the first GWR train left Weymouth with only a few passengers – not surprising as its departure was at 6.15am. It arrived on time at Yeovil, 7.10am. The second train

Interior of the token box on Maiden Newton down platform, 14 June 1988. Author

DMU set B559 calls at Maiden Newton with a train to Weymouth in April 1975. R.A.Lumber

W51066/94 work the 12.00 Bristol (Temple Meads) to Weymouth 24 April 1973. W55027 stands in the bay platform, left, with the 14.20 to Bridport. Author

The decorative
bridge carrying the
drive to
Chantmarle House.
A BR engineer's van
stands on top, 14
June 1988. Author

from Weymouth carried turtles. The first LSWR train from Weymouth did not
leave until 11.55am. The GWR capitalised on the line's opening and ran cheap
excursions to Weymouth, one in April 1857 consisting of 18 coaches carrying a
total of 1,000 passengers.

Regarding an excursion, the LSWR was forced to eat humble pie. On 7
October 1857 the LSWR ran a special train to Weymouth, overlooking the fact
that the Government had declared it a Public Fast Day in memory of the
massacre of Europeans caused by the Indian Mutiny. The running of this train

Grimstone Viaduct,
29 October 1980.
Author

resulted in Lewis Crombie, the LSWR secretary, writing a letter of apology to the editor of the *Southern Times*.

On 26 August 1862 the GWR 2-4-0 *Victoria* ran out of control down Upwey Bank when working the 7.20pm Chipppenham to Weymouth. Before the days of continuous brakes throughout the train, Fireman Carter stood on the frame and sanded the rails to give more adhesion. He jumped off before the engine reached the buffers and injured himself when he struck one of the roof supports. *Victoria* smashed through the buffer stops and ran across King Street, stopping only just short of the Somerset Hotel and giving inspiration for a song written with the refrain 'Victoria in the gin shop'. Carter was severely rebuked by Locomotive Superintendent Daniel Gooch for 'leaving the engine'.

The Lubbock Act of 1871 making four statutory Bank Holidays for workers – Easter, Whitsun, the first Monday in August, and Christmas – gave the Weymouth leisure industry a boost. The *Southern Times* of 11 August 1875 reported that on Bank Holiday Monday that year, 'train after train, laden as it could possibly be, came in rapid succession'.

The railway enabled a different class of passenger to visit Weymouth. In pre-railway days, stage coaches to the town could only carry a maximum of 300 passengers per week and only the professional classes and gentry could afford the time and fare. The railway offered cheap and speedy travel and the number of boarding houses in Weymouth grew from 64 in 1852 to 126 in 1880.

Although the broad gauge offered a more stable and therefore safer ride, with the development of railways in the United Kingdom, it meant that rolling stock from broad gauge lines was unable to run on a standard gauge line and vice versa. The break of gauge caused the time, trouble and expense of transhipping goods, or passengers having to change trains. In due course it was

Grimstone & Frampton, 22 July 1966, view down. The station became unstaffed 11 April 1966 and closed 3 October 1966. The signal box closed 5 April 1966. The building is a typical single storey, uncanopied WSWR structure. Author

Bradford Peverell
& Stratton, view up,
22 July 1966.
Author

thought sensible to convert the WSWR to standard gauge and this task was carried out between 18 and 22 June 1874.

The broad gauge permanent way chiefly consisted of rails on longitudinal sleepers connected by transoms at intervals of 11ft. That design lent itself to fairly easy conversion as the transoms could be cut to suit the narrow gauge and the longitudinal sleepers with rails attached, slewed over to the new gauge. The actual work of conversion could be eased by previously clearing away the ballast and marking the transoms ready for cutting. The platelayers engaged on conversion were drafted in from other districts and were carried on special trains. They received 1s 3d a day for rations and drank oatmeal sweetened with sugar. This drink was distributed in large buckets into which each workman dipped his tin cup. It gave them strength to carry out their arduous task. The GWR provided sheds for the men to sleep in and straw to sleep on, but little rest was taken, 17 or 18 hours being worked out of every 24, for the work was deliberately undertaken during the long summer days.

The previous evening all broad gauge stock was removed from sidings and each stationmaster was required to provide a certificate that his station and district was clear of broad gauge stock. Much of it was eventually broken up at Swindon, though the locomotives were sold for conversion to stationary boilers. The *Somerset & Wiltshire Journal* reported that the new gauge brought new light, roomy and comfortable coaches. The old third class coach was open end to end 'exposing occupants to noise, conversation and effluvia of some 30 passengers, is – it is fondly hoped – gone for ever'. The new coaches, on six wheels, had five compartments and patent buffers which steadied the train and prevented concussion. The second class seats were stuffed and padded, not only for the back, but also the head. First class compartments had gilt mouldings.

To cope with increasing traffic, the line was doubled in 1881. In 1935 it saw some of the first diesel trains in England, but full dieselisation did not come until 6 April 1959. Until 26 September 1959 the Channel Islands boat express ran daily every summer from Paddington to Weymouth Quay while daily services ran to Wolverhampton and Bristol. Much of the Channel Islands market garden produce was also carried over the line – in 1912 124 special potato trains ran

between 1 May and 24 June earning £19,062. Five tomato specials ran daily at the height of the season, while in coal-burning days the Royal Naval ships at Portland required fuelling. With the withdrawal of the Channel Islands boat expresses from the route and also the market garden produce train, the line was used less intensively. It was singled between Yeovil South Junction and Maiden Newton 26 May 1968 and Maiden Newton to Dorchester West on 9 June 1968, Maiden Newton retaining its double track as a crossing loop. In 2002 the former WSWR south of Castle Cary was very much a Cinderella line, but in recent years successful regeneration has occurred. Known as the 'Heart of Wessex Line', it is supported by various highly active groups. Volunteer supporters maintain station gardens to make the environment more attractive. Others produce and distribute simple, local timetables, or arrange guided walks from the stations. All these

Dorchester West, view up, 22 July 1966. Author

The GWR station at Dorchester view north circa 1930. Author's collection

efforts have succeeded in doubling the number of passengers using the line since 2002.

The first station on the WSWR in Dorset was Thornford Bridge Halt opened 23 March 1936.Originally two timber-built platforms, the original up platform was replaced by a concrete platform and shelter transferred from Cattistock Halt when this closed in 1966. About ¼ mile to the south, the War Department's Beer Hackett Sidings serving an Army store, opened 30 September 1942 and were taken out of use on 15 October 1961.

The stone buildings at Yetminster were in the typical WSWR style of architecture but today all the original buildings have been demolished. North of the station two sidings opened in 1932 served a United Dairies' depot. In steam days, passenger trains requiring assistance up the 1 in 51 bank to Evershot were required to stop at Yetminster for a banking engine to be coupled at the rear.

Chetnole Halt opened on 11 September 1933 and like Thornford Bridge, had timber platforms costing £410, but later replaced by one of concrete, in this case coming from Cattistock. Evershot Tunnel, 348yd in length, has very solid looking portals. Evershot differed from other WSWR stations in being of wood. It had water cranes to supply engines dehydrated by the climb to about 500ft above sea level. An unusual feature of Evershot station was that any ordinary passenger train was allowed to be stopped specially for Lord or Lady Ilchester in person, or by their special request, or on an order signed by either of them. Trains could also be stopped for the personal accommodation of Lord Stanondale, the Hon. John Fox-Strangeways, or for Lord Ilchester's agent.

Cattistock Halt opened 3 August 1931 with two timber platforms, was rebuilt with concrete components in 1959, but closed on 3 October 1966. Maiden Newton station had two through roads while a bay platform covered by a timber train shed, was provided for the Bridport branch train. The station building is of knapped flint. The 660yd long Frampton Tunnel was not necessary

Dorchester West in 1965, an example of more elaborate WSWR architecture. J.H.Lucking

No 5940
Whitbourne Hall
works the 4.35pm
Saturdays-only
Weymouth to
Cardiff passing
Dorchester West,
12 August 1961.
R.A. Lumber

Construction work
at Dorchester, view
up circa 1908.
M.J. Tozer
collection

from the engineering point of view, but was made to secure the privacy of the adjoining estate. Grimstone & Frampton station had brick buildings and closed on 3 October 1966. The goods siding was not opened until as late as August 1905. Until then, it was unusual in being a station without a siding. Bradford Peverell & Stratton Halt opened 22 May 1933 with timber platforms,but in 1959 these were replaced by those of concrete. It closed 3 October 1966. To the south is the 66yd long Bradford Peverell Viaduct across the River Frome. Between this viaduct and the 264yd long Poundbury Tunnel, on the south side of the line is a Roman aqueduct and when the WSWR was proposed, the Dorset Field Club under guidance of the poet William Barnes, agitated for the preservation of the historic site.

Dorchester West, designed by Ritson, is a splendid station with round-headed windows. Until 1934 it had an all-over roof. To the south, the LSWR line from Wareham joins, this now being electrified. Came Bridge Halt opened on 1 July 1905 to serve a golf links and two villages. On 1 October 1905 it was renamed Monkton & Came Halt – a less confusing title. Unusually, no waiting shelters were provided. It closed on 7 January 1957. The line descends through

Dorchester Junction 14 June 1988 view up from the front seat of the 13.05 Weymouth to Bristol (Temple Meads) DMU. The electrified double track to Dorchester South curves right, and the single track to Dorchester West and Castle Cary, left. Author

43XX class 2-6-0 No 8329 leaves Upwey Wishing Well Halt in 1938 with auto car No 37. A Weymouth locomotive daily took up duty as Dorchester pilot to shunt the yard and work transfer trips to and from the SR. Normally such a coach was worked by an auto-fitted tank engine. Bincombe South Tunnel is 48yd in length. Author's collection

West Country class Pacific No 34093 *Saunton* banks an up Westbury freight headed by sister engine No 34021 *Dartmoor*, 2 July 1967. Steam working ended the following week. R.A. Lumber

the 814yd long Bincombe Tunnel. One day the 2.10pm Weymouth to Waterloo slipped to a standstill climbing the 1 in 52 through the tunnel and then the weight of the train dragged the engine backwards. Emerging from the tunnel and Bincombe South Tunnel below the Dorchester Road, is a marvellous vista of Weymouth Bay.

Upwey Wishing Well Halt opened on 28 May 1905 to attract tourists. Originally built of timber, in 1946 it was rebuilt in concrete, but all to no avail as it closed on 7 January 1957. Upwey was not originally provided with a station, but following pressure, the GWR agreed to open one if the public subscribed £150. They actually provided £174 2s 0d - £90 3s 6d by Broadwey and £83 18s 6d by Upwey. Built of timber it opened on 21 June 1871 but LSWR trains did not call until 1 February 1872. It closed on 19 April 1886 when Upwey Junction was built about ½ mile to the south to serve the Abbotsbury Railway. Upwey Junction also had timber buildings with the branch platform set at a lower level than the main line. A further curiosity was that the branch platform doubled as the approach road to the main line platforms. Following closure of the Abbotsbury branch on 1 December 1952, the station was renamed Upwey & Broadwey. Radipole Halt, originally of timber, opened on 1 July 1905 to serve an expanding Weymouth suburb. The platforms were replaced by concrete in 1949. It closed officially on 6 February 1984, but because of its condition, for safety reasons, no train had called after 31 December 1983.

Weymouth station was originally a timber structure with overall roof set on a foundation of timber piles. It was designed by J.H.Brereton, engineer to the GWR for eight months after Brunel's death. In World War 2 the glass was removed from the end screens as a precaution in the event of bombing and the overall roof removed in March 1951. The GWR arrival and departure platforms

43XX class 2-6-0 No 6372 climbs out of Weymouth with the Railway Correspondence & Travel Society's 'The Wessex Wyvern'. Revd Alan Newman collection

Upwey Junction, view up. Notice the advertisement for the *Daily Telegraph* below the station nameboard; this was a common feature in the nineteen-thirties. Author's collection

A 1910 LSWR poster advertising Weymouth. Author's collection

Upwey Junction view down circa 1935. The Abbotsbury branch is on the right of the station buildings and joins the main line beyond the shrubbery at the end of the up platform. Author's collection

were in the centre, with the LSWR lines on each side. The original low platforms were later raised by jacks to the standard height. The station was gas lit until October 1976. Life-expired, the station began to be demolished on 13 August 1984 and the new buildings came into use on 3 July 1986. On 16 May 1988 the Waterloo to Weymouth service was electrified. On 26 June 1905 the GWR opened one of the first bus depots in the country. From 22 July 1912 the bus services were run jointly with the LSWR. It was the last bus service to run by railway management and was transferred to the Southern National Omnibus Company on 1 January 1934.

At first the WSWR had a timber-built two-road engine shed. To cope with the growth of traffic, a three-road shed was opened in June 1885. With the withdrawal of steam, it closed on 9 July 1967, the land on which the depot stood being used for constructing a housing estate. The LSWR also had a two-road timber locomotive shed, it facing that of the WSWR. It closed in January 1939 as the site was required for station enlargement and from then onwards, SR engines used the GWR shed.

The GWR was one of the earliest railways to use diesel railcars. A trial run was made to Weymouth on 23 January 1936 and shortly afterwards Weymouth to Bristol Temple Meads received a regular railcar service.

A 'foreigner' south of Upwey Junction. Ex-LMS Class 4 0-6-0 No 44096 from Bath (Green Park) shed, heads a Bath to Weymouth excursion, 10 September 1949. It would have travelled via Broadstone Junction. R.K. Blenkowe

Steam railmotor No 3 at Radipole Halt, view north. Author's collection

The 1.30 pm Waterloo to Weymouth hauled by Merchant Navy class Pacific No 35026 *Lamport & Holt Line*, its nameplate covered as it had not been named officially, passes Weymouth shed, 22 July 1949. Pursey Short

Weymouth station, probably in 1857, the year of its opening. A Hercules class 2-4-0, probably No 40 *Windsor*, is in evidence. Author's collection

A busy scene at Weymouth, 28 June 1924. The GWR was fond of having a wide variety of coaches in its trains. Author's collection

The exterior of Weymouth station, 7 August 1981. The buildings were constructed from timber. Author

West Country class Pacific No 34104 *Bere Alston* heads the 17.35 to Waterloo, 10 April 1965. The removal of the train shed gave the roof an unbalanced appearance. Edwin Wilmshurst

33 119 at Weymouth on 18 July 1979 ready to propel its 4-TC set to Bournemouth where the coaches will be coupled to the rear of an electric unit for the rest of its trip to Waterloo. Author

Electric multiple unit set No 1244 working the 11.53 Weymouth to Bournemouth, 14 June 1988. Author

The new Weymouth station presents a bland appearance on 14 June 1988. Author

A stranger at Weymouth circa 1914. Great Central Railway 4-4-0 No 1038 has arrived with an excursion from the Midlands. Author's collection

The GWR Saint class 4-6-0 No 2933 *Bibury Court* at Weymouth 28 May 1929. This locomotive was withdrawn in January 1953. To its right is the SR T9 class 4-4-0 No 118. The SR locomotive shed in the background closed in 1939 after which SR engines used the GWR shed.   H.C.Casserley

Weymouth locomotive shed following an air raid 17 January 1941. The crane for lifting engines stands out clearly in the background. Author's collection

0-6-0PT No 1367 shunts the sidings opposite the locomotive shed, 22 July 1947. Pursey Short

No 6851 *Hurst Grange* (of Worcester shed) on the turntable at Weymouth shed, 27 August 1950. It is in the early BR black livery with red background to name and number plates. Pursey Short

Merchant Navy class Pacific No 35012 *United States Lines* at Weymouth coaling stage, 11 February 1967, with an ash wagon and piles of ashes nearby. Wagons can be seen beyond the coaling stage. Edwin Wilmshurst

Weymouth locomotive depot, left to right: BR Standard Class 4 2-6-0 No 76003, West Country class Pacifics No 34023 *Blackmoor Vale* and No 34024 *Tamar Valley*, the latter being watered. The photograph was taken on 1 April 1967 – the last day of general steam on the SR. R.A.Lumber

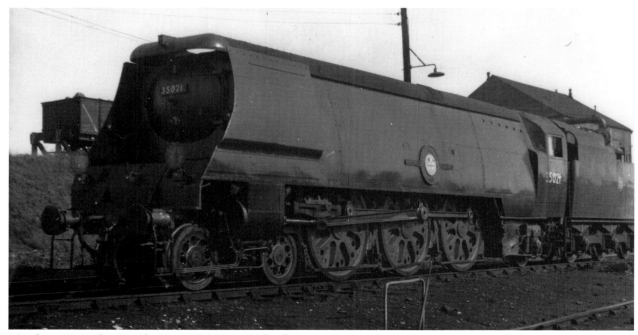

Merchant Navy class Pacific No 35021 *New Zealand* Line at Weymouth, 30 August 1953. Revd Alan Newman

11 Maiden Newton to Bridport & West Bay

FOLLOWING THE passing of the Bridport Railway Act on 5 May 1855 – a very memorable date – the first meeting of the company was held in Bridport at the home of solicitor Edward Gill Flight on 11 May. He was rewarded for his hospitality by being appointed secretary of the company and premises in East Street were rented from him for £400 a year. Scotsman Henry Johnston Wylie was appointed engineer and a fellow Scotsman, Kenneth Mathieson, the contractor. Joseph Gundry, chairman of the company, cut the first sod on 19 June 1855 at Loders, midway between Bridport and Powerstock. In July, at the

Maiden Newton view down circa 1910, with the train shed covering the Bridport branch bay platform, right. The platform on the left is of timber. Author's collection

Maiden Newton view down, 24 April 1973; the train shed over the bay platform has been removed and the metal trellis footbridge been replaced by one of concrete. The 12.00 Bristol (Temple Meads) to Weymouth is on the left and the connecting 14.20 Maiden Newton to Bridport, right. Author

Maiden Newton view down, 15 September 1950. Following the arrival of a train from Bridport, the coaches are reversed into the siding on which the single coach stands. The engine is then uncoupled and run to the parallel line. The guard then releases the coaches' brakes and the vehicles gravitate to the bay platform. The engine then backs on to what is now the front of the train ready for the return to Bridport. R.A. Lumber

Toller station, 22 July 1966. Author

first general meeting shareholders were told that the line would cost £65,000. Hopes were expressed that the railway would be opened by the autumn of 1856, but such desires were over-ambitious.

The greatest earthwork was at Witherstone and the contractor experienced difficulty with the earth slipping – in fact one of the slips required the purchase of extra land from a Mr Jenkins. He granted permission but with the proviso that a siding would be laid for his use.

James Gerrard built Bridport station at a cost of £1,300. It had an overall roof until 1894 when a down platform was built which also provided a run-round loop and obviated the need for horses to draw the passenger coaches to the platform. Inexpensive stations were opened at Powerstock (£260 10s 0d) and Toller, the company threatening to close them should they prove unremunerative. Powerstock station was shrewdly built like a cottage so that in the event of it not proving economic as a station, it could be used as a dwelling. Existing cottages near Bridport station were renovated for habitation by porters, the engine driver and stationmaster. The 9¼ miles of broad gauge line opened on 12 November 1857, the day being declared a public holiday. Such a vast crowd turned up to travel on the inaugural train that the stationmaster did not finish issuing the tickets until 30 minutes after its scheduled departure. This resulted in passengers missing the connection at Maiden Newton.

Unlike most contemporary stations which were lit by oil lamps, Bridport and Powerstock were illuminated by naptha gas supplied by the railway

The cottage-like
station at
Powerstock, 22
July 1966. Author

Bridport circa 1958 with the engine shed, left (it closed 15 June 1959) and goods shed, right, which closed 5 April 1965. The signal box closed 8 June 1965. Lens of Sutton

company. Initially the line was plagued by trespassers and for a brief period two men were employed at 3s 6d a day to warn people off the line. Certainly some folk in the district were far from law-abiding. On Boxing Day 1857 vandals placed iron rails across the track at Toller; on 8 January 1858 a large stone was placed on the line at Bridport and on 14 April 1858 just over a shilling in cash was stolen from Powerstock station while the stationmaster was attending church.

Within twelve months of opening, a further serious slip occurred at Witherstone and drainage works were required. No less than 20,000 cubic yards of spoil had to be removed, but it was discovered that it was eminently suited for brick making, so was disposed of at a profit. Together with the WSWR, the branch was converted from broad to standard gauge between 18 and 22 June 1874.

A train arriving at Bridport in August 1957. The signalman has collected the single line staff from the fireman and is walking back to his box. Another 0-6-0PT and passenger train stand on the right. The 'Bridport' sign is in SR green enamel. Edwin Wilmshurst

The Bridport Railway retained its independence longer than most local companies and it was not until 1 July 1901 that the GWR purchased it, paying £6 cash for every £10 Bridport Railway share.

It was anticipated that an extension to Bridport Harbour would benefit dividends so on 21 July 1879 an Act was passed, the GWR agreeing to subscribe £12,000 towards the cost of construction. The new line was built by Messrs Mousley & Lovatt and on 23 February 1883, to assist with the line's construction, the contractor's locomotive was driven along the highway from Bridport station to Bridport Harbour, six horses assisting it around bends, its fixed wheelbase not being conducive to rounding curves.

Bridport circa 1906. The track is of bridge rail laid on longitudinal sleepers. The down platform has a substantial shelter – though following the withdrawal of passenger services to West Bay, only a small shelter was really required on the arrival platform as the only people needing to use it were those waiting to meet passengers. Author's collection

The line opened to traffic on 31 March 1884 when no less than 5,100 passengers travelled over the extension. This figure included 1,100 Sunday School children who were bitterly disappointed when, due to wet weather, they were not allowed out of the train and were taken back to Bridport. A thatched cottage at East Street, Bridport, was economically converted to a combined stationmaster's house, booking office and waiting room. In due course, before the building could go up in flames, the GWR replaced this thatched cottage with a standard design brick station and stationmaster's house, the work being carried out by J. & H. Childs, a local contractor. Hoping to encourage tourists, Bridport Harbour was renamed 'West Bay' by the railway, but in the event did not succeed in ousting Weymouth as watering place.

The Bridport branch proved vital to the World War Two war effort. Millions of hemp lanyards were used by the services, sometimes 300 tons despatched at a time. 50,000 hay nets for Army horses were sent off weekly, in addition to rifle 'pull-throughs', tent, balloon and airship ropes, camouflage nets and twine for stitching canvas. Steel cord was used for producing anti-submarine indicator nets, the largest of which measured 300ft by 180ft. Vast quantities of timber were needed for the war and some trees felled locally, were brought to the running line and loaded there, rather than being taken to a station siding. Passenger services on the West Bay extension were withdrawn temporarily

Bridport
locomotive shed
circa 1952. At the
foot of the water
column a brazier
with a tall chimney
keeps the contents
of the water tank
from freezing in
cold weather.
Author's collection

between 1 January 1916 and 1 June 1923 and then, due to bus competition, withdrawn permanently on 22 September 1930, goods traffic continuing to use the line until 3 December 1962.

The opening passenger service of 5 trains each way daily between Maiden Newton and Bridport took about 35 minutes to cover the 11¼ miles and by 1938 the 11 down and 10 up trains were allowed 18 minutes. Passsenger trains over the whole branch were restricted to 40mph, with a further reduction to 10mph through Powerstock and on the West Bay extension. Engines were stabled in the single track shed at Bridport until it was closed in June 1959 having been rendered redundant by dieselisation.

In the nineteen-thirties the GWR introduced Camp Coaches. These were old vehicles converted for cooking and sleeping; crockery, cutlery and bedding being

Bridport view up
showing the
departure platform,
signal box and
goods shed circa
1958. Author's
collection

supplied. In 1935 one camp coach was stabled at West Bay and the following year another placed at Powerstock.

World War Two had its effect on the branch. On 4 November 1940 sidings at Bradpole and Loders were opened to stable railway wagon-mounted Howitzers capable of firing a 750lb shell a distance of about eight miles. These sidings remained in use until 22 April 1945 by which date the threat of invasion had diminished. During World War Two train loads of shingle were taken from West Bay for use in airfield construction, while trainloads of nets were despatched.

Bridport looking sadly neglected, 10 October 1970. 'Excursion' is displayed on the DMU's destination linen. The crossing in the foreground is made from old sleepers. Edwin Wilmshurst

In 1949 the average number of passengers using the branch daily amounted to 137 in winter and 340 in summer. Despite Toller and Powerstock stations becoming unstaffed on 11 April 1966 (platform lamps being sent from Maiden Newton daily and returned by the guard of the last passenger train) the branch proved uneconomic to operate and was closed completely on 5 May 1975, exactly 120 years to the day of the passing of the Bridport Railway Act. Track lifting began on 18 November 1975. When the Bridport trains were replaced by a bus, within a few weeks the operator found that, typically, traffic had fallen to a quarter of its initial level; that the operation was therefore uneconomic and so the service was withdrawn.

Toller station still exists. The original building went up in flames on 12 October 1902 when the accident-prone stationmaster caused a paraffin lamp to explode. Reconstructed in timber and brick in June 1905, this building may now be seen at Littlehempston, the South Devon Railway's station at Totnes.

Although the railway was less susceptible to snow than roads, occasional problems were encountered. The blizzard of 1881 blocked the branch and the last train from Maiden Newton on 18 January did not arrive at Bridport until next morning and the following three days' service was drastically curtailed. Ten years later, on 10 March 1891, snow blocked the line near Powerstock and was not cleared until 12 March. 26 December 1886 saw severe flooding in the Bridport and West Bay area: a bridge was washed away near Toller and another near Bradpole weakened. Bridport to Maiden Newton trains re-started in 31 December, but could not run through to West Bay until 3 January.

An 0-6-0ST,
believed to be No
2115, approaches
Bridport East Street
circa 1907. The
stationmaster's
house built in 1904,
can be seen on the
left. Author's
collection

Bridport East Street
view down circa
1958. Lens of
Sutton

West Bay viewed
from the East Cliff
circa 1910. On the
left are cattle pens,
while on the right
quite a few wagons
are loaded with
timber, probably
part of a ship's
cargo. A motor car
stands by the gate.
Author's collection

12 **The Abbotsbury Branch**

IN 1872 an Act of Parliament was applied for to build a branch from the main line at Upwey to Abbotsbury. In addition to carrying the usual items, it was anticipated that it would transport millions of tons of iron ore from Abbotsbury where it lay close to the surface and could easily be extracted. Another expected traffic was Portland and Purbeck stone from Portesham (pronounced 'Possam'). Following strong opposition from an influential local landowner, the Bill was withdrawn.

The idea was not forgotten and a successful application was made in 1877. William Clarke was appointed to draw plans and sections. Clarke's first railway appointment had been with the Shrewsbury & Crewe Railway, then from 1859-1862 he was resident engineer of the Lahore Division of the Punjab Railway. In 1863 he completed the Tenbury & Bewdley Railway and the Ludlow & Clee

The Abbotsbury branch platform at Upwey Junction circa 1935; the main line platforms are beyond the fence on the right. Notice the steep downwards gradient. Author's collection

Upwey Junction, the Abbotsbury branch is on the left. An SR train to Weymouth approaches. Notice the neatly-kept platforms. M.J.Tozer collection

Hill Mineral Railway. In May 1866 he became a member of the Institute of Civil Engineers and that same year was appointed assistant chief engineer of the London & North Western Railway. In 1870 he was engineer to the Bristol & North Somerset Railway constructing a line between Bristol and Radstock. He is particularly known for his station buildings, all of a similar design.

The contract for building the Abbotsbury branch was placed with Monk & Edwards in May 1879, the firm immediately starting construction. Unfortunately two fatalities occurred in October that year when a fall of earth east of Portesham trapped a couple of men between the cutting and a spoil wagon. A collection was made for the deceased married man, and £30 to £40 given to his widow and four children.

Only a quarter of the company's capital was subscribed, so Monk & Edwards stopped work in April 1880. In April 1882 Messrs Green & Burleigh

Upwey Junction circa 1947. The board at the head of the 1 in 44 gradient reads: All Down Goods & Mineral Trains Must STOP DEAD Here'. The curve has a 10 chains radius. J.H.Russell

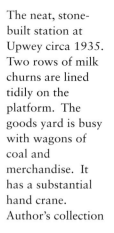

The neat, stone-built station at Upwey circa 1935. Two rows of milk churns are lined tidily on the platform. The goods yard is busy with wagons of coal and merchandise. It has a substantial hand crane. Author's collection

Upwey station in sad condition on 11 February 1967 following track-lifting. Edwin Wilmshurst

Smartly-dressed passengers leave Abbotsbury station circa 1910 having arrived in the steam railmotor. Cattle trucks can just be seen at the far end of the station beyond the shrubbery. Author's collection

undertook to complete the line and all the capital had been subscribed by March 1884, over a half of it by the contractor. Ill-fated, the firm had overstretched itself, stopped work in October 1884 and was declared bankrupt the following March.

Some of the navvies working on one of the contracts were black. A ship carrying them had been wrecked and, instead of returning directly to the USA, they obtained work building the Abbotsbury branch. In the twentieth century, Negro spirituals learned from them were still sung in local public houses.

On 16 December 1884 the contract was taken over by George Barclay Bruce of Westminster, a civil engineer largely concerned with Indian railways. He became President of the Institution of Civil Engineers in 1887 and was knighted the following year. Bruce took over Green & Burleigh's shares and construction work restarted in January 1885. In April 1885 a locomotive arrived at Portesham to assist with the construction. It had been drawn along the public highways by a traction engine. While quarrying for ballast, oil shale was discovered and believed to have commercial potential. The station buildings were constructed by subcontractor Edwin Snook of Broadwey and all were situated on the left-hand side of the line proceeding towards Abbotsbury. The line, worked by the GWR, opened with little ceremony on 9 November 1885.

517 class 0-4-2T No 561 at Abbotsbury with two auto trailers plus a van to accommodate the considerable milk traffic. Author's collection

1947 view to the goods shed. The goods yard does not appear to be over-busy. It closed 1 December 1952. J.H.Russell

The expected heavy mineral traffic failed to materialise. The supposed iron ore field at Abbotsbury turned out to be merely Kimmeridge clay, and the stone traffic did not develop as expected, but in 1888 the engineer, George Bruce, the company's principal shareholder, formed the Portesham Quarries Company to develop the stone workings. He also proposed extending the Portesham tramway, built by William Mansfield in 1885 to connect the quarry with Portesham station, up to the Ridgeway to gravel pits near the Hardy Monument. Bruce's attempts failed and the line was disused by 1897.

The Abbotsbury Railway failed to make a profit and was sold to the GWR on 1 July 1896. Early in the twentieth century the GWR economised by replacing all branch signal boxes with ground frames, saving on both maintenance and wages.

Apart from the ordinary traffic of the district, including quite a lot of milk churns (Friar Waddon milk platform opened north of Coryates about 1932 and closed in 1939) the only other consignments were small quantities of locally caught mackerel, but these stopped about 1930. With the development of road transport, the line became unprofitable and most of it closed to passengers and freight on 1 December 1952, though freight continued to run from Upwey Junction to Upwey until 1 January 1962, the branch station having the only goods depot in the area, as Upwey Junction catered solely for passengers. The railway would have been more popular with passengers had the plan for a more central site for Abbotsbury station not met with opposition. In 1949 the average number of passengers on each of the 13 daily winter trains was just over five and on the 14 summer trains, 8½ .

In June 1917 in order to reduce the tonnage of imported oil, supplies of which were threatened by German submarines, shale was excavated by German prisoners of war brought daily from their camp at Dorchester. Wagons were loaded at Corton Siding, opened half a mile east of Coryates Halt. This siding was out of use by September 1921 as, despite efforts, the main shale bed had still not been reached. Coryates opened on 1 May 1906 had a 14in high platform at first before eventually being raised to standard height. Its shelter had part of its front wall removed to accommodate milk churns.

Abbotsbury had a stone built locomotive shed which closed in September 1894 after which the branch engine was supplied by Weymouth shed. The water tank at Abbotsbury was filled by removing an engine's whistle and attaching a flexible pipe to a steam pump.

517 class 0-4-2T No 531 at Abbotsbury circa 1907 hauling a nearly new auto trailer, probably No 37. Author's collection

The roofless engine shed at Abbotsbury in 1947; it had closed back in 1906. The stone base of the adjoining water tower contained a steam pump powered via a flexible hose which was temporarily connected in the place of a locomotive's whistle. In the distance is the goods shed which closed 1 December 1952. J.H. Russell

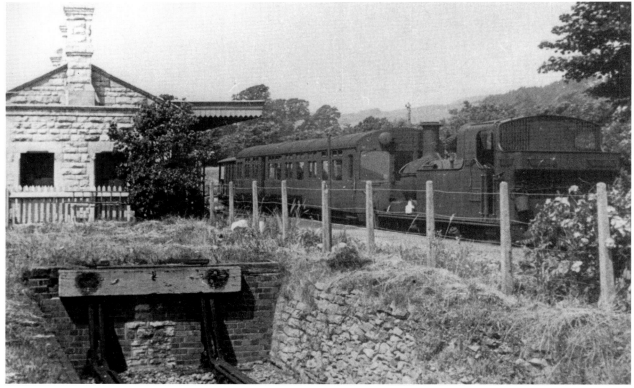

0-4-2T No 1454 and auto trailer at Abbotsbury, 1947. On the left is the end loading dock which appears to have seen little recent use. J.H. Russell

13 Weymouth Quay Tramway

0-6-0ST No 1337 *Hook Norton* at Weymouth 1906, standing just inside the yard gates. It was purchased by the GWR in 1904 from the liquidators of the Hook Norton Ironstone Partnership Ltd. In front of the airy cab notice the warning bell for use on the tramway. A tow rope is draped over the smoke box door handles. To the right of the engine are milk vans and a loading gauge. The engine was withdrawn and cut up in January 1926. M.J.Tozer collection

PROBABLY THE most fascinating line in Dorset is the Weymouth Quay Tramway where full-sized engines and rolling stock travel for about a mile along public roads linking the station with the harbour.

The mixed gauge line opened to goods traffic on 16 October 1865, the wagons drawn by horses. The LSWR never exercised its running powers so the standard gauge was not used initially. Following conversion of the WSWR in June 1874, the standard gauge rails of the tramway were used for the first time. Adoption of standard gauge helped develop the importation of Jersey potatoes

0-6-0T No 1376 or 1377 passing the Portland Hotel circa 1904 and about to enter the goods yard. The portion of the Backwater seen on the right was later reclaimed. Author's collection

0-6-0ST No 2195 *Cwm Mawr*, an ex-Burry Port & Gwendraeth Valley Railway locomotive, hauling a passenger train along the tramway. Notice the two flagmen ready to control road traffic. Author's collection

to the Midlands and the North, as wagons could run straight through without transhipment. In 1876 3,500 tons of this commodity were carried.

On 19 March 1878 members of Weymouth Corporation were taken on a trial trip along the tramway in a coach hauled by a steam engine. The Act of 30 June 1862 under which it was built stated that only horse power could be used, so the Corporation's permission was required for locomotive working. Following the trip this was granted and a locomotive was probably first used regularly on 7 June 1880, but horses were still used for minor shunts until 1931. Although the line was maintained by the GWR, it was actually the property of the Corporation. In the early days the Corporation offered the tramway to the GWR for £20 – barely the cost of conveyance – but it was rejected. The GWR took over the Channel Islands shipping service on 1 July 1889 and on 4 August 1889 the tramway was opened to passenger trains.

0-6-0PT No 1367 passing below Town Bridge with an express to Paddington, 22 July 1949. Pursey Short

The sharpest curve used by passenger trains in Dorset, 223ft radius, was at Ferry's Corner. To prevent buffer interlocking there, special couplings had to be used between bogie passenger coaches. Each of the three links was 16in long instead of the normal 12in. This meant that each passenger vehicle had to be uncoupled from its neighbour and the special coupling attached. Although the real purpose was to prevent buffer locking, there was the added advantage that these loose couplings gave a small engine some assistance when starting, as it could start from rest adding one coach at a time until all the couplings were taut. When corridor stock appeared in 1891, the corridor gangways had to be disconnected and the doors locked to prevent any wandering passengers falling between the coaches.

By 1908 as many as 300 wagons were dealt with daily and because of the short shelf-life of flowers, new potatoes and tomatoes from the Channel Islands, and broccoli and other vegetables from France, rapid transport was essential. Inevitably during transfer from ship to rail some damage occurred and local boys scavenged broken boxes of tomatoes and split potato sacks.

As fitting the special couplings cost time and money, in the nineteen-thirties the curve at Ferry's Corner was eased to a radius of 400ft and this widened the

0-6-0~PT No 1370 with a goods train, 10 March 1955. John Bamsey

Boat train hauled by diesel No 2197, 12 August 1972. Notice the combined warning bell and flasher unit in front of the radiator. Edwin Wilmshurst

quay by 70ft. Due to World War Two the Channel Islands services ceased in 1940, but the quay remained open for military traffic. A train ferry terminal for use by the SR's *Hampton Ferry* and *Shepperton Ferry* was constructed in 1943 by the Royal Engineers and situated immediately before the cargo stage ready for the invasion of France, but in the event it was never used. After the war the quay was reopened to goods on 18 September 1945 and to passengers on 15 June 1946. Owing to the large amount of cargo for the Channel Islands in 1959, much of the outgoing freight was taken to Portland for sorting and checking before going to Weymouth Quay for shipment. The last PERPOT (perishables and potatoes) train ran in 1970 and the quay closed to goods in February 1971, the Channel Islands service being transferred to Southampton. Although in the early sixties five boat trains were required on summer Saturdays, traffic then seriously declined. Regular passenger services ceased on 26 September 1987 and since this date only specials have used the tramway.

On 22 July 1966 D2043 stands while a container is unloaded from a wagon to a German ship. Here it is possible to lean out of a bedroom window and shake hands with passengers in a passing train. Author

Tomatoes being unloaded from the cargo TSS *Pembroke*, September 1921. Author's collection

Rebuilding the wall September 1938. Author's collection

(Top) 0-6-0PT No 1368 on Custom House Quay with a perishables train June 1955. The warning bell can be seen above the running plate immediately in front of the cab. Author's collection

2R 21778/16

THIS TRAIN RUNS ALONG THE PUBLIC ROADWAY BETWEEN THE QUAY AND THE JUNCTION WITH THE MAIN LINE AT WEYMOUTH. PASSENGERS ARE ASKED NOT TO USE THE LAVATORIES DURING THIS PART OF THE JOURNEY.

(Middle) The label fixed to passenger coaches using the tramway. Author's collection

(Bottom) Four coaches at Weymouth Quay in its single track days. Author's collection

0-6-0ST No 2194 *Kidwelly*, ex- Burry Port & Gwendraeth Valley Railway, at Weymouth Quay station in 1935. Mail sacks are on the extreme left. Author's collection

33 111 buffering up before heading a boat train to Waterloo, 5 August 1974. Note the bell and flasher above the buffer beam. R.A.Lumber

0-6-0ST No 2195 *Cwm Mawr* at Weymouth Quay. Author's collection

0-6-0PT No 1367 at Weymouth Quay 25 June 1949. A Stothert & Pitt crane built at Bath shows in the top right hand corner. Revd. Alan Newman

14 The Somerset & Dorset Joint Railway

THIS WELL-LOVED line began as the Dorset Central Railway, the remnant of a scheme for linking the Midland Railway at Mangotsfield, just north of Bristol, with Poole. The DCR Act for building a line from Wimborne to Blandford received Royal Assent on 29 July 1856. Next the DCR put forward a Bill to extend its line northwards to Bruton there to link with the Somerset Central Railway and make through communication between Poole and Highbridge. The section from Wimborne to Blandford was opened 1 November 1860 and two years later, the extensions from Glastonbury to Bruton and

Stalbridge view down circa 1964. Its roof rather dwarfs the walls. The gas lamp, left, has an old rail as part of its base. Note the pull wires for turning it on or off. C.Steane

133

4-4-0 No 71 in dark blue livery, heads a down train at Stalbridge circa 1920. Just 'SD' on the buffer beam was unusual - 'SDJR' was general. Author's collection

Templecombe to Bruton opened on 3 February 1862. The DCR and the SCR amalgamated that same year, the combined companies being called the Somerset & Dorset Railway. The new company took for its seal a design incorporating a train passing Glastonbury Abbey and Tor, and the Arms of Dorchester. In 1863 the S&D opened the final stretch between the English Channel and the Bristol Channel. Although the S&D ran ferry services across to Cardiff and Cherbourg, not many passengers wished to avail themselves of this facility.

The company was in a poor state financially and the challenging idea was put forward which was hoped would prove to be the company's salvation. This was an extension over the Mendips from Evercreech Junction to Bath where a connection would be made with the Midland Railway, thus making it part of an

important through route between the North and South. This extension opened on 20 July 1874 and from this date Bournemouth to Bath became the main line. Construction of the extension had exhausted the company financially and it needed to be purchased by a larger company. While the GWR and Bristol & Exeter were having a drawn-out discussion on the matter, the Midland Railway and the LSWR nipped in and secured the line jointly on a 999 year lease.

They successfully developed traffic and the line proved vitally important during both World Wars carrying men and arms to the south coast. The line was particularly busy on summer Saturdays, down trains which deposited holidaymakers at Bournemouth early in the morning, returning with home-going passengers. All through passenger trains to and from the North were withdrawn

The water tank at Sturminster Newton circa 1966. Notice the 'devil' to prevent freezing and the long leather bag which a fireman places in a locomotive's water tank. The water gauge situated on the end of the tank is inoperative as the float and pointer are missing. C.Steane

BR Standard Class 9 2-10-0 No 92220 *Evening Star* leaves Sturminster Newton with an up train, 30 September 1963. Revd Alan Newman

Stourpaine & Durweston Halt, view up, 4 May 1963. The concrete components were cast at Exmouth Junction. Author

at the end of the summer of 1962, only the local stopping service remaining. This alone proved uneconomic and all passenger traffic was withdrawn on 7 March 1966 and most of the line closed.

Until 1 January 1930 the S&D had its own blue livery for locomotives and coaches, but after that date, engines were taken into LMS stock and painted in that company's style while the coaches were painted SR green. For those unaware of the company's history, it was a surprise to see an LMS engine at Bournemouth as, geographically speaking, the resort could hardly be described as London, Midland, or Scottish.

Travelling from Bournemouth to Bath via Wimborne involved a reversal and loss of time uncoupling the locomotive and running round the train. This irritation was avoided by building a 3 mile long cut-off from Corfe Mullen to Broadstone. This was opened to goods traffic on 14 December 1885 and to passengers on 1 November 1886.

In the twenties and thirties, the railway's running costs increased due to higher wages and more expensive coal, while the development of road transport

siphoned off a certain amount of traffic. The passenger service – only one train a day – to Wimborne, was withdrawn on 11 July 1920, as was goods traffic on 17 June 1934. except for the section from Corfe Mullen to Carter's clay siding which remained open until 19 September 1959.

The S&D had a staff lodging house at Wimborne

A porter pushes a laden trolley at Blandford Forum circa 1966. C.Steane/Author's collection

with a resident steward who catered for the footplate crews and guards who rested there. Opened in February 1902 it was a model rest house with hot and cold running water – a facility many of the men lacked in their own homes. The lodging house closed 1 December 1922 and the locomotive shed itself on 22 January 1923.

The interior of
Blandford Forum
goods shed circa
1966, showing a
wide variety of
goods carried by
the railway. The
platform has been
raised.
C.Steane/Author's
collection

The S&D offices at
Blandford Forum.
Author's collection

BR Standard Class 9 2-10-0 No 92220 *Evening Star* heads an up train at Blandford Forum, 30 September 1963. Revd Alan Newman

An interloper on the S&D: ex-GWR 0-6-0PT No 3720 at Blandford Forum, 30 September 1963. A bucket for crew washing was often hung on the rear bunker. Revd Alan Newman

S&D 4-4-0 No 17 at Blandford Forum, its paintwork in splendid condition. Author's collection

BR Standard Class 5 4-6-0 No 73054 at Blandford Forum on the 09.03 Bristol (Temple Meads) to Bournemouth West, 9 January 1965. The name board has the addition 'For Bryanston School'. E.T.Gill

Adapting an overbridge to span double track near Blandford, 3 May 1900. BRB(R)

A derailment at the above overbridge, 6 March 1929. S. Sealy, District Controller, Bath, is on the right; H.H. Whitaker, District locomotive Superintendent in charge of the Bath breakdown gang stands in the four foot wearing a bowler hat. Notice the newer brickwork on the right. Author's collection

Ex-S&D Class 4 0-6-0 No 44558 heads the 1.10 pm Bournemouth West to Bristol (Temple Meads) at Charlton Marshall, 4 May 1963. Author

A down train hauled by a 0-4-4T approaches Spetisbury circa 1900. Dr. T.F Budden

The new station building being erected at Spetisbury circa 1901. Double track opened on 29 April 1901. The disc and crossbar signal is prominent. Author's collection

Spetisbury view up circa 1910, showing the new down platform and line opened 29 April 1901. The small signal box can be seen at the end of the platform. Author's collection

The site of Spetisbury station, view up, 4 May 1963. It was reduced to a halt on 13 August 1934 and closed 17 September 1956. Author

Ex- S&D Class 7F 2-8-0 No 53807 heads a semi-fast train near Spetisbury, 3 July 1954. R.E.Toop/Author's collection

Bailey Gate from the north circa 1900. Author's collection

Bailey Gate station and the milk factory circa 1966. C.Steane/Author's collection

Six-wheel milk tankers at Bailey Gate creamery, circa 1966. C.Steane/Author's collection

Class 2 4-4-0 No 40634 at Corfe Mullen Junction working the 12.23 pm Bristol (Temple Meads) to Bournemouth West, 20 January 1962. The line on the right leads to Carter's Siding and formerly to Wimborne. Edwin Wilmshurst.

Corfe Mullen Junction signal box view down circa 1966. '25' is a speed restriction sign. C.Steane/Author's collection

Corfe Mullen halt circa 1966. C Steane/Author's collection

Carter's siding circa 1966. C. Steane/Author's collection

BR Standard Class 4 4-6-0 No 75027 near Broadstone Junction, July 1960. Author's collection

S&D 4-4-0 No 67 approaches Broadstone Junction station with a down express. Notice the sand-drag, left, which would halt a diverted runaway. Author's collection

Broadstone Junction view up, 4 May 1963. The S&D curves left beyond the signal box while the SR keeps straight ahead to Wimborne. Author

Broadstone station view up circa 1910. Author's collection

Broadstone, view towards Poole, circa 1966. C.Steane/Author's collection

S&D 0-6-0 No 76 at Broadstone heading an express. Author's collection

BR Standard Class 4 4-6-0 No 75072 heads an up S&D goods through Broadstone, 4 May 1963. Author

Class 4F 0-6-0 No 44417 approaches Broadstone Junction with an up S&D goods train from Poole. Colin Roberts collection

S&D 0-4-4T No 55 near Broadstone 1914. Author's collection

The utilitarian Creekmore Halt, view towards Poole, circa 1963. Lens of Sutton

15 Narrow Gauge Lines

$\mathbf{I}$N ADDITION to broad and standard gauge lines, there were some narrow gauge railways in Dorset, the most extensive of these being in the Isle of Purbeck where three systems existed. The horse-worked Middlebere Plateway built in 1806, ran from Norden pipe clay pits to a staithe at Middlebere Creek. Instead of rails it had cast iron plates 3ft in length, the vertical and horizontal sides each measuring 3in. They were attached to stone sleepers by oak plugs. The line was probably abandoned circa 1907.

Fayle's Tramway was a 5¾ mile long 3ft 9in gauge system built in 1905 from the Norden Pits to Goathorn Pier. It was worked by steam locomotives, one

being *Tiny* , a 0-4-0T built by Stephen Lewin at Poole circa 1875. The short line to Goathorn Pier closed circa 1939. Although really an industrial railway, after closure of the school at Goathorn, between 1920 and 1936, about ten children of the clay workers were conveyed to and from Corfe in a saloon, virtually a shed attached to a flat truck. Dorset County Council paid for this passenger service. Following the closure of the Goathorn Pier line, the remaining section was relaid to a gauge of 1ft 11½in. One of the engines used was the ex-Welsh Highland Railway 2-6-2T *Russell.* The line ceased operation in 1972. The bridge carrying the line to the transhipment siding with the Swanage branch can still be seen today east of Norden station.

The primitive, but effective catch points protecting runaways from crossing the A351, 29 August 1968. Part of an R.Hudson wagon is on the left. Author

Pike's Tramway, a 2ft 8½ in gauge line opened circa 1866 was worked by steam engines all with Latin names, but latterly, internal-combustion engined locomotives were used. The line ran from Furzebrook to a wharf on the River Frome. Unlike most narrow gauge railways which used a combined central buffer and coupling, Pike's Tramway used the standard two-buffer arrangement. The line closed in 1956.

The Swanage Pier standard gauge tramway ⅓ mile in length, opened in 1858,was designed by Capt W. Moorsom, chief engineer of the Southampton & Dorchester Railway. It was later converted to 2ft 6in gauge. It principally carried stone to barges, and latterly coal for ships' bunkers. Fish were also carried and the occasional corpse from a shipwreck. Sections of the line can still be traced today.

Another railway not open to the public is that operated by Sylvasprings, a line for carrying watercress at Doddings Farm, Bere Regis.

Bogie wagons loaded with gorse at the exchange siding, Norden, 29 August 1968. Author

0-4-0 diesel-mechanical Orenstein & Koppel locomotive on Fayle's Tramway, 29 August 1968. Author

Ruston & Hornsby 4-wheel diesel-mechanical locomotive on Fayle's Tramway, 29 August 1968. Author

A loaded train leaves the watercress beds at Dodding's Farm, Bere Regis, 24 April 1973. The 4-wheel petrol-mechanical locomotive built by Jesty in 1948 is powered by an Austin 7 engine. The gauge is 1 ft 6in. Author

A train en route between the watercress beds and the packing station, 24 April 1973. Author

Suggested Further Reading

Atthill, R, *The Somerset & Dorset Railway* (David & Charles, 1967)

Baker, M, *The Waterloo to Weymouth Line* (Patrick Stephens, 1987)

Barrie, D S & Clinker, C R, *The Somerset & Dorset Railway* (Oakwood Press, 1948)

Beale, G, *The Weymouth Harbour Tramway in the Steam Era* (Wild Swan Publications, 2001)

Bradshaw's Railway Guide August 1887; April 1910; July 1922; July 1938 (David & Charles reprint)

Bradshaw's Railway Manual, Shareholders' Guide and Directory, 1869 (David & Charles reprint)

Brown, P A, *Many and Great Inconveniences: the Level Crossings and Gatekeepers' Cottages of the Southampton & Dorchester Railway* (South Western Circle, 2003)

Clark, R H, *An Historical Survey of Selected Great Western Railway Stations* (Oxford Publishing Company, volume 1 1976, volume 2 1979, volume 3 1981)

Clinker, C R, *Register of Closed Passenger Stations and Goods Depots 1830 – 1977* (Avon Anglia 1988)

Cooke, R A, and G A Pryer, *Track Layout Diagrams of the Great Western Railway and BR Western Region Section 17* (Author, 1983)

Cox, J G, *Castleman's Corkscrew, The Southampton & Dorchester Railway 1844 – 1848* (City of Southampton, 1975)

Faulkner, J N, & Williams, R A, *The LSWR in the Twentieth Century* (David & Charles, 1988)

Fay, S, *The Royal Road* (EP Publications reprint, 1973)

Gosling, T, & Clement, M, *Dorset Railways* (Sutton Publishing, 1999)

Hateley, R, *Industrial Railways of South Western England* (Industrial Railways Society, 1977)

Hawkings, M, *The Somerset & Dorset: Then & Now* (David & Charles, *1995*)

Jackson, B L, *The Abbotsbury Branch* (Wild Swan Publications, 1989)

Jackson, B L, *Isle of Portland Railways* (Oakwood Press, Vol 1 1999, Vols 2 & 3 2000)

Jackson, B L, *Yeovil, 150 Years of Railways* (Oakwood Press, 2003)

Jackson, B L, & Tattershall, M J, *The Bridport Railway* (Oakwood Press, 1998)

Judge, C W, & Potts, C R, *The Somerset & Dorset Railway: An Historical Survey* (Oxford Publishing Company, 1979)

Karau, P, *Great Western Branch Line Terminii Volume 2* (Oxford Publishing Company, 1978)

Kidner, R W, *Railways of Purbeck* (Oakwood Press, 2000)

Lucking, J H, *Dorset Railways* (Dorset Press, 1982)

Lucking, J H, *Railways of Dorset* (RCTS, 1968)

Lucking, J H, *The Great Western at Weymouth* (David & Charles, 1971)

Lucking, J H, *The Weymouth Harbour Tramway* (Oxford Publishing Company, 1986)

MacDermot, E T, revised Clinker, C R, *History of the Great Western Railway* (Ian Allan, 1964)

Maggs, C G, *Branch Lines of Dorset* (Sutton Publishing, 1996)

Maggs, C G, *The Bath to Weymouth Line* (Oakwood Press, 1982)

Maggs, C G, *The Last Years of the Somerset & Dorset* (Ian Allan, 1991)

Maggs, C G, *Somerset & Dorset: Life on the Bath to Bournemouth Line* (Ian Allan, 2007)

Marsh, J, & Webb, M, *The Rise & Fall of Wimborne Station* (Buggleskelly Books, 2004)

Mitchell, V, & Smith, K, (all published by Middleton Press)

    Bournemouth to Evercreech Junction 1987
    Yeovil to Dorchester, including the Bridport Branch 1990
    Bournemouth to Weymouth 1988
    Branches Around Wimborne 1992
    Salisbury to Yeovil 1992
    Branch Lines Around Weymouth 1989
    Branch Line to Swanage 1986
    Branch Line to Lyme Regis 1987
    Dorset & Somerset Narrow Gauge 2006

Nicholas, J, & Reeve, G, *Main Line to the West; Part Two: Salisbury to Yeovil* (Irwell Press, 2007)

Nock, O S, *History of the Great Western Railway vol 3* (Ian Allan, 1969)

Oakley, M, *Discover Dorset Railway Stations* (Dovecot Press, 2001)

Peters, I, *The Somerset & Dorset* (Oxford Publishing Company, 1994)

Phillips, D, *The Westbury to Weymouth Line* (Oxford Publishing Company, 1994)

Phillips, D, & Pryer, G, *The Salisbury to Exeter Line* (Oxford Publishing Company, 1997)

Phillips, D, *From Salisbury to Exeter: The Branch Lines* (Oxford Publishing Company, 2000)

Popplewell, L, *Bournemouth Railway History* (Dorset Publishing Co,1973)

Potts, C, *An Historical Survey of Selected Great Western Railway Stations* vol 4 (Oxford Publishing Co, 1985)

Pryer, G A, & Paul, A V, *Track Layout Diagrams of the Southern Railway and BR SR Section S1, S3 & S5* (R.A. Cooke, 1980, 1981, 1982)

Read, P R, *Powerstock Station – All Change* (Author, 1996)

Reeve, G, & Hawkins, C, *Branch Lines of the Southern Railway, vol 1* (Wild Swan, 1980)

Robertson, K, *Great Western Railway Halts, vol 1* (Irwell Press, 1990),vol 2 (KRB Publications 2002)

Rose, E J, *The Axminster to Lyme Regis Railway* (Kingfisher, 1982)

Ruegg, L H, *The Salisbury & Yeovil Railway* (David & Charles reprint 1980)

Smith, M, *Railways of the Isle of Portland* (Irwell Press, 1997)

Smith, M & Reeve, G, *The Story of the Lyme Regis Branch* (Irwell Press, 2003)

Stone, C, *Rails to Poole Harbour* (Oakwood Press, 1999)

Tavender, L, *The Dorchester & Southampton Line* (Ringwood Papers,1995)

Thomas, D St J, *Regional History of the Railways of Great Britain: vol 1, The West Country* (David & Charles, 1981)

White, H P, *Regional History of the Railways of Great Britain: vol 2, Southern England* (David & Charles, 1970)

Williams, R A, *The London & South Western Railway, vols 1 & 2* (David & Charles, 1968 & 1973)